I0137381

Yesterday
When I Was
Crazy

A Sacred Contract
With Healing

PAULA POTTS, RCST, BCPP

TAKE
CHARGE
BOOKS

Brevard, North Carolina

Published by:
Take Charge Books
Brevard, NC

Copyright © 2017 Paula Potts

All rights reserved. Except as permitted under the United States
Copyright Act of 1976, no part of this publication in any format,
electronic or physical, may be reproduced or distributed, in any
form or by any means, or stored in a database or retrieval system
without the prior written permission of the publisher.

ISBN: 978-0-9982658-2-7

Editor: Kathleen Barnes

Cover and interior design: Gary A. Rosenberg
www.TheBookCouple.com

Printed in the United States of America

Contents

This book is dedicated to my beloved daughter, Sylver.

Sylver Logan Sharp, her name is music to my ears! She single-handedly championed my sacred contract with healing from the beginning of my fall into disability and despair until the present. She loved me enough to believe in me and to care for me at every turn of events no matter how shocking or life shattering.

Sylver is the joy of my life and more than I could have ever hoped for in a daughter. My favorite saying as we grew up together was, *I always knew why God gave me a child.*

When *crazy* started to define my spirit and I was unable to represent myself to the powers that be, Sylver willingly took on all my survival challenges with vigor and love. Whether negotiating my case with government officials or with doctors in clinics or in a hospital emergency room, she was loyal and brave throughout all I endured. When I went from the hospital to the polarity therapy classroom, she never once questioned my choices or called me crazy. She took on family, friends, skeptics and all who stood in the way of her mother's recovery.

Imagine if you will, trying to make sense out of illnesses that doctors did not understand and could not name much less treat. Imagine watching your mother going crazy, having panic attacks and screaming out loud and crawling on the floor after painful treatments day in and day out not just for months, but for years.

Sylver was a budding young star embarking on an amazing journey as a vocalist when these tragic circumstances took over our lives in the early 90s. Just as I was losing touch with reality, losing my job and my life force, she was called to become the lead singer of the legendary band, CHIC. She miraculously fulfilled her destiny and watched over her ailing mother without any obvious signs of discouragement or determent.

I am filled with gratitude for a benevolent creator who brought Sylver into the world through me and gave me her spirit to share. Words are insufficient to express my appreciation for her faith in me. In 2014, she still watches over me like an enduring angel.

There's more! She brought me doggies! Three miniature Schnauzers—Foster, the first; Aria, his wife; and Blanche, their offspring—are also guardians of my sacred contract with healing.

Introduction

*L*OVE IS THE ANSWER! THIS IS THE MORAL OF THE STORY I am telling in this book. It is what I know for sure. A smile in the eyes of an ailing friend when she sees my face, a shift in perception when it seems all is lost, the adoring arms of a lover when only touch matters—are all ways love answers us.

Forgiveness, compassion, support, to name a few, all are expressions of loving-kindness. More important, they are instruments of God's healing grace and mercy. The Soul knows this! Thanks to the alignment of quantum physics and metaphysics in the 21st century, mankind can know the healing power of what I call "lovingness" more than ever before. Together Spirit and Science see the path ahead as full of potential and possibilities for healing all over the world as our hearts and feelings take the lead. Now we know! Now we love!

So this is a book about Love and Healing. It is about how these two ideas are intertwined. My goal is for you to experience this miraculous union in your life—especially when you need it the most. I did. It saved my life!

Love is the answer is my guiding principle in 2014. I needed to learn this to rebuild my life. In the early 90s, an avalanche of injuries that resulted in severe physical illness and complete emotional deterioration struck me.

At age 40, I was diagnosed with fibromyalgia—the pain that never stops. In my prime and at the height of my career, I was forced to abandon my life's work and my lifestyle as I knew it. Everything changed.

At first, everything changed for the worse. For seven long years, my medical conditions got increasingly more severe and debilitating.

My dis-ease grew exponentially as I added the diagnoses of depression, dysthymia, cold sensitivity and even dissociation.

My days and months and hours were filled with the agonies of pain, overmedication, immobility, fibro fog, isolation, panic attacks and visits to the emergency room. My outlook on life was bleak and cloudy. At my worst, I hated my body and my life and feared for my future to the point of self-loathing and raging anger.

For the most part, medical practitioners and even friends thought the pain in my body was "all in my head." I was "just crazy" for suggesting that the pain never stopped. Who would believe such a thing? Crazy was a catchword for unexplainable, stressed-out, female behavior. *You know how women are? Always complaining about things that don't exist . . .* sound familiar? Sorry fellas! I had to get that off my chest!

Then one day I would learn another universal truth, *God Is Bigger.* I wrote a poem with this title in 2005 as the revelation became abundantly clear. There was a new horizon emerging in my soul that held the promise of God to heal my life. A sacred contract with healing was unfolding that would begin my journey to wholeness and health building.

My hope for recovery was found in the little known field of *energy medicine.* The "new age" healing process that changed my life forever, started in a dance class. This is where I would learn about

Dr. Randolph Stone and his amazing, holistic energy healing system, polarity therapy.

I will share more about my experiences with *energy medicine* treatments later in this book. In the meantime, suffice it to say, the results were miraculous! For over ten years, my everyday life was focused on a strategically measured, full-time healing regimen. Many alternatives were tried, including supplements, essential oils and even tuning forks. From sunrise to sunset, I focused all of my time on a diet and exercise routine.

So my most important message is, I did the work! I stretched and juiced and did breathing exercises and energy exercises and all sorts of healing work for over a decade . . . as if my life depended on it! It did!

As my sacred contract with healing took hold, it gave new meaning and purpose to my life. This book is about the work I did both in and out of the treatment room to reclaim my health and my passion for living. I dedicate my writing to helping others find the path to their sacred contract with healing. I believe we all have such a path.

Central to this love story is a relationship with *gifts of the Spirit*—perhaps my greatest source of inspiration. So you are probably asking, "What do you mean, 'gifts of the Spirit'?" Mostly I am talking about prayer, intuition, journeying, clairvoyance, divination, angels and all the "invisible" means by which we access information, direction and even grace. I learned that *gifts of the Spirit* have a way of bearing fruit.

Love came in on the wings of healing touch, tireless faith, determination and angels all around. Self-love replaced self-hatred. Courage and conviction pioneered my divinely ordered journey to self-healing. Crazy became the tale of *yesterday's* woes and sorrows. Passion and promise called forth a future filled with balance and harmony.

I am honored to share my story of love and healing. I am called to remind all who will listen:

God is bigger!
Bigger yet,
More than otherwise
You can get.
Forever faithful,
Loyal and true.
God's power can build your dreams for you.

Love is the answer—I can say that from deep within. This book tells all about it from my heart and my pen.

—Paula Potts
Washington, D.C., June 2014

CHAPTER 1

The Veil Is Lifted

P ERHAPS I SHOULD INTRODUCE MYSELF AS I AM IN JUNE 2014 before I share the story of who I have been for the past couple of decades. This will give you, dear reader, greater context and perhaps it will make the contrasts more poignant.

At age 65, I am well and whole, way beyond my wildest imaginings. I have pioneered my way through a sacred contract with healing with both curious and miraculous results. I am still manifesting my soul's destiny with my new life as a storyteller. Chronic dis-ease and disability have become my greatest teachers and my most abiding inspirations. Spreading the "good news" about *energy medicine* has become my life's purpose.

To those who have known me for the past 25 years, I am the victim of severe physical and emotional disorders who found miraculous healing. Many witnesses can now attest to my remarkable adaptation to a healing process that no one knew anything about when I signed into a Synergy-Dance class in 1993. In the depths of my despair, I was seeking relief and rehabilitation in familiar places the best way I knew how.

I had no prior knowledge of energy healing before then. I had taken dance classes from age 4 through adulthood. But it was the normal kind of dance: ballet and tap, modern and ethnic. My "dancer legs" were among my greatest assets. They kept me fit and toned and having fun. I absolutely love to dance!

Fibromyalgia stole this joy from me in the early years of severe pain and disability. I, who reveled in my dancing shoes, walked with a cane for several years due to debilitating back pain. I only wore flat shoes. I could stand up for only short periods of time because my muscles became so weak. Sometimes I crawled up the stairs, grateful that they were carpeted. I could not lift my arms to brush my hair much less hold fifth position like a proper ballerina.

A prominent rheumatologist's prognosis was that I would "probably never dance again." That was a staggering blow. I am certain that remark sparked my ultimate determination to leave no stone unturned in my quest for wholeness.

Little did I know during those seemingly endless painful days that my dancing ability would be one of my greatest comforts and inspirations to move forward. Dance was the gateway to my healing process. I was introduced to polarity therapy in a SynergyDance class. I will say more about how I got to this turning point later in the book.

Now I can dance and run (a little) and even wear my "tipping shoes" when I want to feel like the belle of the ball. My journey into the unknown world of energy healing is finally accepted as having value. The "secrets" of my decades of alternative therapies are out. However, only a few of my dearest and closest family and friends are privy to the how of my mysterious healing process until now, when I have chosen to share these wonders with all of you.

Energy medicine? What is that? Over and over I've been asked this question by those who listened to my stories of healing from dis-eases. At least finally I was being asked about it. For so long, no one asked. Most people just stared at me with perplexed looks in their eyes.

I did not speak publicly about my treatment process very often. The unfamiliarity of it all was too much to explain and too much to grasp. Inquiring minds really did not want to know. The idea of energy medicine was too sensational, not to mention suspect. The dawning of the "energy age" was just on the brink of its emergence as the new science of the 21st century.

To make bad matters worse to most observers, I was training as a practitioner in this thing called *energy medicine.* I was serious, too! Or perhaps I was just *crazy*! To put a cherry on top, I credited this work with saving my life. Now, so many people in my life decided that I was really off the deep end!

Sadly, the label of "crazy" was all too familiar in my life. My early childhood and young adult life were fraught with challenges with emotional trauma and feelings of being overwhelmed. The outward signs of my inner turmoil often looked "crazy." So I was not daunted by the disdain or the unbelief that I encountered. I knew it to be lack of knowledge and understanding of my circumstances. I was used to folks saying, "That's just Paula! You know she is just crazy!"

Truth be told, I did not understand very much when I started my studies in polarity therapy, the health-building paradigm founded by Dr. Randolph Stone. I had never heard of anything even remotely similar until my very first SynergyDance class. What I believe now is that my Spirit knew that energy medicine was not only the call of destiny but also my soul's divinely ordered ministry.

So who I am now is the high priestess of my own soul. I live and breathe self-healing principles and practices daily. As a truth seeker in 2014, I give thanks hourly for all the blessings of my life. I am free to tell my stories and pray for healing for all people everywhere.

My resume includes polarity therapist, craniosacral therapist, choir member, author, poet and jewelry designer. Best of all, I am back stage mommy to an incredibly gifted daughter who is the joy of my existence. Several generations of very special mini-Schnauzers share this joy as my loving companions and constant healers. It is fair to say that sometimes I do not recognize myself.

What is most important to say about who I am in 2014 is that I am on a mission. I live a passionate desire to pioneer the healing potential of energy medicine to the glory of God.

Who I Was

Those who knew me between the ages of 30 and 40 would describe a very different person than they would see today. They would most probably use terms like "high achiever," "power broker," "Type A," "no nonsense," "perfectionist" and "social butterfly," just to list a few.

As a young, higher education professional employed at the U.S. Department of Education in Washington, D.C., I was following my family tradition. The passion for education is in my DNA. As the daughter of a college president, it was perfectly normal that I would be the one to get the job done well and then get the kudos. I was fulfilling the call of my heritage.

For the most part, I enjoyed serving the cause of higher education in general. I was particularly grateful for the opportunity to help Historically Black Colleges and Universities (HBCUs). I moved to the nation's capital in 1975 to do just that as a research associate of the R. R. Moton Memorial Institute. It was good for family continuity and harmony. My father was a highly regarded HBCU president for most of my early life in Denmark, South Carolina. I grew up on a college campus, which was a bountiful experience!

Notwithstanding my successful tenure of service as a bureaucrat, I languished in a less-than-nourishing environment. Promotions and popularity came to a halt when I became disabled with fibromyalgia, the mythical medical disorder, in 1988.

The pursuit of "reasonable accommodation" as a disabled employee became the bane of my existence. Air conditioning became my enemy. The label, "crazy" came back to haunt me. The die was cast! People again would whisper, "That's justPaula! You know she is just crazy!"

My supervisors began to think their talented, dynamic employee was more trouble than she was worth.

Few people believed that I was sick. I was thought to be acting out from too much stress. Several persons in authority over my employment status accused me of "using my gifted brain to get over." Some thought I was manipulating the system since I was well versed in policies and procedures. I was considered to be faking the pain so I did not have to work. After all, no one could be in pain "all the time." The judgment was swift, emphatic and unsympathetic.

I was too smart for my own good. All the clichés were applied. There was very little compassion for my tales of pain and suffering. As you can imagine, these earth-shattering betrayals would ultimately make me crazier than I had ever been before. The fall from grace would be long and devastating to every facet of my being and my life.

In 1992, I retired from the federal service on disability after an arduous two-year battle that involved voluminous medical reports and Congressional interventions.

My cycle of trauma was complete. A bedridden, emotional cripple, I was disenfranchised from life as I knew it. My integrity defiled and degraded, I was, in the words of Elizabeth Lesser, "broken open" and pleading for mercy. My career ended abruptly as did my young marriage to my second husband. My soul was fractured and dreading what looked like a very bleak future.

Childhood

So continuing with the historical time line from birth to age 29 takes me back in time to the 1950s and '60s in South Carolina where I was known as the president's daughter, one of those Potts girls. There were three Potts sisters, and I was in the middle. We also had an older sister, who was adopted by my family when she was a teenager. She was away in college most of our young life. The four sisters had one brother, the pride and joy of our generation.

My parents were well known and highly respected all over the state. There was no hiding out or slipping and sliding. The distinguished reputation of my family followed me everywhere. In the good ol' days, neighbors and friends were watching and telling our folks if we were caught out of order. The Potts girls were always under surveillance.

Privilege is the best word to describe my upbringing anyway you look at it. Living in the "big house" always had the look of royalty. The President's House at the college where I grew up had just such glistening trappings. Our highly esteemed dwelling was resplendent with double living rooms with mirrored walls and a dining room with murals and bureaus laden with silver services. Add a crew of housekeepers and grounds keepers and the image of these regal surroundings is complete.

Just so happened that I was born into what some call "Negro Royalty." It was certainly the black bourgeoisie, if you ask author and sociologist, Dr. E. Franklin Frazier. There are pedigreed genes on both sides of my family tree. For generations, my ancestors pursued laudable callings and causes, including their own higher education and the education of our race. Everybody in my family spoke "standard English" like a college professor's offspring should. From birth we ate, slept, drank and oozed language and learning, math and science and arts and humanities.

My fathers and mothers rose above the terrorism of slavery to become landowners, physicians, educators and humanitarians dedicated to making life better for the less fortunate.

There was also a strain of musicality that was passed on through the generations. It is a birthright to be cherished. We were also endowed with a profoundly deep reverence for the Earth and all of nature. Many of my family members have the gift of gardening and growing beautiful flowers and trees. I would be the novice in that gardening talent pool.

Yet, all these blessings and gifts and talents would pale in comparison to the envy they precipitated in my early life. As a result of these many advantages, I was the most hated girl in school, or so I thought. For most of my early years, I pretty much hated being the president's daughter. I was bullied and picked on daily in school. It did not help that I was also the smartest kid in the class from first grade through high school.

Valedictory was no prize in my mind. It just made the curse of privilege worse. The well-known phrase, "kids can be cruel" is an understatement in my experience.

The *piece de resistance,* my light-skinned blackness, created my most damning identity crisis as a child growing up in a small Southern town. Silky hair did not make me popular among the girls who relied on hot pressing combs to straighten and style their hair. The boys just wanted to be with the president's daughter for trophy value.

It probably did not help that not only was I academically at the top of the class, I was also a really good singer, dancer and actress. I performed musicals and solos regularly and won prizes at drama festivals. I could play the piano and even won the title of homecoming queen and Miss Honor Society. Somehow, stacking layers of stars in my crown, I persevered. I accomplished great things.

Paradoxically, most of the time, I felt ostracized and friendless. It was almost impossible to know who liked me for me or whether they were using me for my family's status. Simultaneously, I became embroiled in deep sadness, self-hatred and a need to be heard and understood that plagued most of my adult life.

My college life as a vocal music major on scholarship ended abruptly when a series of health challenges forced me to leave school in my freshman year in 1966.

I returned to my college studies a semester later as an English major at Voorhees College. I would ultimately complete a master's degree in education research at the University of South Carolina.

The most significant event in my life occurred during my undergraduate college years when my daughter was born. I was just 19 years old. The marriage to her father was short lived. My marriage to her stepfather had the same fate.

My ability to engage in a healthy relationship was severely impaired by my failed marriages. It would take another 20 years for me to marry again. And I was soon divorced for a third time. (I married the same man twice, 20 years later.) My health crisis had a lot to do with the end of that third marriage.

I was a very successful single mother in spite of these early trials with a good partnership. My daughter is the light of my life and has always held that sacred space with beauty, love and grace. She also championed my healing process, as you will soon learn more about.

Changing the scenery once more in this opening narrative takes us back a little farther in time to my seaport birthplace of Charleston, South Carolina. There are probably few left today who knew me on 54 Montague Street. From 1948 to 1954, our palatial home on the campus of Avery Institute was the dominant force in my family life. My father was school principal. My mother reigned as a stellar first lady. Together they ranked at the apex of all of Charleston's professional and social circles of note.

Langston Hughes was a guest in our house the month I was born. My favorite book is an autographed copy of his poetry book, *The Dreamkeeper*, signed on August 14, 1948—four days after my birth.

The Potts children were the darlings of Charleston society. Our four-story home was larger than life as was our daily bread. We had a basement and an attic and bedrooms large enough for snorers to coexist peaceably. We had a housekeeper along with household help to assist my mother. As a preschooler, I attended a private Episcopal Church kindergarten.

My father traveled often, much to my chagrin. My incessant crying for daddy created tension in my relationship with my mother, according to one of our long-time babysitters. I do not remember these details personally. I am guessing they dwell in places I would like to forget.

The day that this same babysitter of my childhood remarked that she was surprised that I turned out so well and had a nice child, too, was cathartic for me. In that startling moment, I was clueless about the origins of her commentary. It was her first time meeting my daughter, who was eight years old at the time. She had not seen me either in a long time.

Miss Belle, I will call her, admired the earrings I was wearing, which I promptly gave to her. She replied, "I cannot believe you turned out to be generous, too." Being cast as a "bad little girl" in her mind meant I had to be selfish as well. Sorry, it just wasn't so!

My sister, Camille, was visiting with us that day. She recently reminded me that she witnessed the whole event. She further recalled that she heard our former babysitter echo the same account of how surprised she was that I "turned out so well" several times more after that day.

As Miss Belle told the story of my mother and me, she said, "You always wanted to go with your daddy, and it made your mother mad." I gazed intently into her authoritarian eyes as she gave me a look that said, "Listen up!" Her lips pursed, head cocked sideways and hands akimbo, she continued, "You always acted out. We had a time with you when your daddy was away."

She also said that I was called "the little actress," but with little affection. I was aghast! I did not recall any of it, but everything she said made perfect sense. Miss Belle's Southern sass sealed the deal. The "Daddy's girl" label got so much clearer.

Looking back on my childhood impressions now, I can see how my siblings might have been really perplexed by the smart one who was always acting out or sickly. I was that girl! I remember fainting in the school lunch line and catching every virus and the measles and mumps and Chicken pox—twice my mother said. I was given enough penicillin for ten children and would end up allergic to it in my adult years. Then there were the summers where mosquito bites left me covered in calamine lotion, making me a laughing stock in the family and in the neighborhood. Even the bugs seemed to persecute me!

And yet I was somehow the stage princess with a knack for singing and dancing and acting and all sorts of creative expressions. I imagine these facets of my experience engendered some sibling rivalry. Holding the lead role in every production must have been just a little daunting and probably irritating to all those around me.

I was never quite sure about anybody, I guess. At a very young age, I learned not to trust anyone and to hate my otherwise star-studded life. More often than not, I felt despised and alone and unwanted. *How could I be so good at everything and yet so hated?* The "A" student was not equipped to understand any of this. There was no merit or joy in being "the one to beat." I never learned to be competitive, only to be myself.

Moving from our idyllic city life in prestigious Charleston society to rural life in the dairy town of Denmark, I am sure, did not help my status in the family or the world. I was six years old at the time and had already been promoted to the second grade.

My parents and siblings and I were the rare light-skinned black family in town. We looked out of place. I, most often, felt displaced. So the "Potts were stirred" by many things—pun intended.

The babysitter's story was just the tip of the iceberg. I was branded the family's black sheep, a tag that persisted throughout my early upbringing and my adolescent years.

Going crazy when my daddy left was just the beginning of the larger story. It was a very early childhood foible that I lived to regret for decades. But now I know that the black sheep syndrome is one of my greatest teachers. How else could I be separated from the norm just enough to help me find an unknown path to follow as my life's work? The polarity that balances and harmonizes my sacred contract with healing today is filled with such compelling events.

So the label of "crazy" came and went throughout my life. Sometimes it came all the way in and stole my soul's life force. Sometimes "crazy" was just a fit of confusion. All too often, the incidents that gave life to "crazy" were traumatic and overwhelming to my nervous system. The fractures piled up over time. When the dam broke, my life as I knew it was no more. I would have to start over and over and over to regain my health, my dignity and my purpose.

In 2005, I wrote my signature theme poem, *justPaula,* which sheds a little light on my journey to God. The setting for this poetic inspiration is a gossip session among the "green-eyed" bullies until, at last, the *Aha!* moment grips them all. Here's how it goes:

justPaula

Oh, that's justPaula.
You can treat her any ole way.
She's a sucker any day.
Privileged and smart too.
"We really don't like you!"

So it is okay to disrespect,
What we don't appreciate.
And forget to call,
Or just be late.
She won't care. She better not!
Certainly not with all she's got.
So we can do whatever we please.
Doesn't matter if it is really mean.
Oh, that's justPaula.
She's got it all.
Looks and talents and hair that falls.
And when she tries most anything,
Lands the title and wins and wins.
Singer, dancer, writer, the gall—
Why is her ladder of success so tall?
Oh, that's justPaula.
Didn't you know.
It's only because . . .
God loves her so!

You will find many references to justPaula in this book. By way of contrasts, she is not only a multifaceted metaphor for the crazy-girl in my yesterdays but also my greatest inspiration as a poetess. My first poetry book, published in 2009, is entitled, *justPaula: A Few Words—Inside the Mind of Panic, Pain and Healing.* Many of my friends and associates in the world of blog talk radio enjoy this tag as a social media identity that distinguishes my brand of "poetry that heals." I love it!

On a broader scale, justPaula, signifies my place on common ground with all people everywhere. I may be considered pretty, smart and privileged as badges of honor that create advantages that are not available to individuals without these attributes. However, these descriptions of who I am are essentially cultural, categorical demographics devised primarily to provide a context for research and study of social status in our society. The emphasis that is placed on these labels assigned to the human condition keeps us "in the box"—constantly judging one another and competing against each other for the Golden Fleece.

The perceived advantages that accrue from good looks and economic status are part of the mythology of our heritage of hierarchy. "It ain't necessarily so," the song tells us in *Porgy and Bess*. Both the "haves" and the "have nots" live through struggles, successes and seasons they would like to forget. Just watch Tyler Perry's hit show and see this truism in action.

What I am trying to say here is that "I am one" and only *one* soul, living the same 24-hour cycles as everyone else. Storms have literally blown the roof off my house! The gold at the end of the rainbow has shone just in the nick of time when I thought there was no hope of sanity or salvation. I have rebuked haters and had great lovers. Sound familiar?

Like most folks, in the words of Langston Hughes, "Life for me ain't been no crystal stair." If I am special in the annals of history, it is because I am a good steward of at least some of the blessings that I was born into. Going just a step further, I have been gifted with grace beyond measure. I believe grace is available to everyone.

So I am justPaula because I am just like you. I have potential and possibilities and the promises of God—just like you.

Where I am going

It is my good fortune that crazy was not bigger than God. When the poetess was born in 2005 during the ravages of Hurricane Katrina, I penned the poem, *God Is Bigger*. It was the ultimate message from my Spirit. My soul was suddenly free to tell my story. Later that year, *Yesterday When I Was CRAZY* was birthed, first as a poem. I knew instantly, thanks to spiritual muscle testing (more about that later), that this would be the title of my book. I knew for sure that for every yesterday, the sunrise held the promise of tomorrow.

In 2014 I have no regrets! I understand that there are no accidents or mistakes, just lessons and opportunities for a shift in perception, behavior or both. I know that every Soul's journey requires great mastery and trust in something greater than the Self. And while this brave new world of life lessons is not always rosy when crazy is in control, I know yesterday's tattered memories fuel today's healing Light.

I am honored to share my sacred contract with healing with you. It is my greatest gift with responsibilities at this new crossroads in my ever-evolving trek through this lifetime.

So one last cliff-hanger brings me to the end of this opening chapter with another special awakening that charted my dynamic healing process. "Gifts with responsibilities" is a phrase I formed to underscore my belief about the talents we are born with and how we must use them all to heal our lives.

As my stories about self-healing are told, you will see that there were many miracles nesting inside my ritual talents. Dancing, singing, writing, reading, studying—all the things I could do so well—were as great healers as any bodywork session I received. I engaged them all at one time or another in my healing process with as much vigor and expectation for deep transformation as I could muster. I soon understood that I am "responsible" to use my gifts to the Glory of God—it is why I have them!

The later chapters in this book highlight the scope of this amazing awareness that my gifts are my responsibility. These gifts are a major part of the love inside that heals. Only God could have been that clever. Now we must follow suit!

In 2014, I am going my way! The veil of yesterday is lifted; the Light of tomorrow is shining brightly. I am following my dreams and my embodiment of spiritual muscle testing. I am honing my gifts with responsibilities as I continue to expand my horizons. I am writing my stories about love and healing and my walk with God. I pray you are going my way, too. Or better yet, *your* way.

CHAPTER 2

Born Angry

I T IS, INDEED, A BRAVE IDEA TO CONSIDER THAT ONE MIGHT be born angry. It is perhaps equally courageous to consider that a soul would make such a choice as its next passage through time. Did my soul choose to create fibromyalgia? I don't think so, but perhaps. What a theory! Is my cloak of anger the cumulative effect of lifetimes of earthly tragedies destined to yield an endless cycle of human hardships? Or maybe my soul just has a big ego!

Is it possible that many who suffer greatly were just born angry from the act of challenged conception? Now, there is an idea! No, it is rather another truth of our earthly existence. Humans do seem to have cause to act out the rage of abuse and torture for generations of soul incarnations.

Consider the descendants of African slaves who endured the most heinous forms of human debasement for decades. Their off-spring could surely be "born angry" from cellular memory. The con-troversial idea that cells of the body retain memories of our histories raises great skepticism for most people. Growing up as a Negro in the segregated South, I believe my "born angry" story could surely begin and end there in my cellular ancestry. But that would be too easy.

My poem, *Already Angry,* captures the impact of the anger-laden

DNA of African-Americans in the United States. I wrote this poem as I was hanging up from a very stressful conversation with a friend. I realized that my anger meter was on nine about to hit ten. In a moment of self-preservation, I was gripped by the thought: *I am already angry. So I can't get mad.* The poem continues:

I am already angry.
For things in my past
That crushed my soul
And gave my heart a blast
Now I wear an indelible mask.

Is angry behavior essential to our spiritual evolution or self-limiting to our soul satisfaction? Ask yourself this question. Then let your soul answer.

I write this book to say that it is time to heal our layers of anger regardless of their source. Our greatest human experiment just might be to give our souls a little rest from such hard work. Imagine a world with fewer dis-eases and distortions. Imagine forgiveness as everyone's very first response in an offending situation. Imagine an angst-free soul with an earthly assignment without such heavy baggage. In the meantime, I will share my born angry saga and how it saved my soul.

Born again?

In the mid '90s, I was introduced to the concept of rebirthing. It was very early in my studies in polarity therapy. I heard about rebirthing in many encounters with fellow students in my energy medicine classes. For a long time, I knew of this New Age idea as an amazing concept only, not as a therapeutic protocol. I was admittedly skeptical at first. I did not know much about birth trauma either, so I guess rebirthing had no context for me at that time.

I had secondhand information only, no personal stories and no related training. No one I knew had had a rebirthing experience. I heard it through the grapevine of my camaraderie with intuitives and healing arts practitioners who mentioned it from time to time. I could say it was a lingering curiosity among my peers.

In 2014, rebirthing-breathwork, as it is more accurately described, is a powerful healing process that I have researched and experienced personally. I have met several rebirthers who tout the work highly.

Rebirthing therapy consists mainly of constant, connected, conscious breathing in a safe, supportive environment. Founder, Leonard Orr, a New Age pioneer, established the practice of rebirthing in the United States in the 1970s. This natural treatment process provides an opportunity to cleanse or clear unresolved birth traumas from the energy body.

In recent years, birth trauma has become more widely recognized as having causal relationships to many medical disorders. I learned about some of the frequently occurring causes in a class on birth dynamics while I was completing my studies in craniosacral therapy (CST) in the late '90s. I was stunned by the potential for some forms of induced birth to impact physical health and lead to digestive and structural challenges.

Rebirthing-breathwork is a therapeutic gem, known to effect remarkable healing for many sufferers whose dis-eases are not responsive to traditional medical treatments. Reported results of the practice of this work range from the sensation of well being to the release of deeply held trauma to the elimination of medical symptoms, including chronic pain.

Some practitioners have compared the increase in prana in the body attributed to conscious breathing to the sensation of Divine Love. *Prana* is an ancient Sanskrit word for the "life force" or primary essence within all living things. This vital energy is said to move in the cerebrospinal fluid as a conductor to all cells like a living cosmic breath. Prana is often equated with the movement of Spirit in the body.

Many complimentary modalities offer several approaches to rebirthing. There are specific trainings for rebirthers and their guides. All of my personal experiences with rebirthing occurred spontaneously over the two decades of my healing journey. An avid conscious breather, I believe it is my discipline of breathwork that opened the doorway to these rebirthing events.

I learned the practice of progressive relaxation breathing early in my medical treatment process. A skilled psychometrist at the National Rehabilitation Hospital spent three months with me, breaking through my cycles of panic by teaching me the tool of conscious breathing. For over 20 years, conscious breathing has been my anchor in the storm as well as a daily discipline. So what I am learning is that my long experience with breathwork makes me a natural rebirther.

I have had four remarkable rebirthing experiences that I can with confidence state that I was born again in some life-changing way. A true change in perception occurred that defined my forward progress. In her book, *A Course in Miracles,* Marianne Williamson calls this kind of perceptual shift a miracle.

Lodie leads the way

I embraced my first rebirthing miracle in the care of a special friend and fellow practitioner of Polarity Therapy. Lodie, I will call her, had a deeply intuitive resonance in the realm of Native American healing arts. Our session was imbued with symbolism and sounds that reflected her native attunement. Sacred totems of all kinds held the space.

I had always been proud of my native ancestry. Although there was some uncertainty with regard to the exact tribal affiliation, I was raised with an understanding that one of my great, great grandmothers and one of my great, great grandfathers was of Native American descent. Whether Blackfoot or Mohawk, my parents did not seem to know for sure. Documentation of such facts for African-Americans was hard to come by. It didn't matter to me. I loved that part of myself probably because I could see my great-greats in the mirror every time I gazed upon my long, bone straight hair.

One of my fondest memories of our family mountain home in North Carolina is of a visit to the Cherokee Village to see the play, *Unto These Hills.* Richly tanned from the summer sun, my mother and I were asked by a Cherokee woman to identify our tribal connection. "What tribe are you from?" she inquired. We smiled, grateful for the recognition and acceptance.

So Lodie and I were uniquely bonded for what our native inspired session would reveal. We were open to discovery in our work together.

I assumed my place on the treatment table, and Lodie did her thing. What started out as just another polarity practice session turned into a potent opportunity for healing unlike any other I had known. It was an anointed day of delving beyond the veil.

About midway through the session, I shifted into a fetal position. A cycle of squirming and moaning and crying poured forth with force and intention. Suddenly I knew that I was feeling myself back in my mother's womb waiting to be born. Somehow I also knew that I was crying out for help.

Lodie inquired as to my distress. I cried out, "I don't want to come out! I don't want to come out! Please, I want to stay in here! I don't want to come out!"

I remember the sounds and movements of my anguish as I flailed around on the table for what seemed like an eternity. An unborn soul not wanting to be born: How could this be me? Why was I saying this? What was I afraid of?

When I came back to my self after Lodie's expert grounding techniques, I knew I had experienced a miracle. From that day forward, I recognized that I never wanted to be born into the world. One soul secret had been unveiled. I was catapulted into a journey of discovery that would take years to reveal the whole truth about my soul birth.

I was perplexed and yet purged of a dark sadness. I was gifted with a new beginning. I was born again!

Believe it or not

Admittedly, what I have just recounted is in the category of "unbelievable" for most Americans and maybe even most people. Although other cultures find comfort in just such journeying, metaphysics is not truly the American way. I believe introspection takes many forms. Healing can be just around the corner of an open mind and heart. But it is thinking outside the box.

Twenty-five years ago, no one believed me when I said I was in pain. Except for my personal physician, Dr. R. George Adams, and just a few close family and friends, I was labeled a liar and a fraud. When I was diagnosed by Dr. Reynolds in 1988, fibromyalgia was a virtual unknown. The "pain that never stops" was just as unbelievable as the incredible story I just told about rebirthing. Panic attacks were just crazy people acting out. People like me were advised to "Get over it."

For the first seven years of my illness, I lived and moved in a sea of suspicious glances and condemning eyes peering into my very soul. This demeaning experience alone could have been the ultimate betrayal that ended my journey to the Light. The anger that built up in my gut around the humiliation from my peers could have been the end of my potential for healing right from the beginning. "You couldn't be in that much pain, not all the time," the unbelievers chanted at every opportunity.

Then came rage! The indignation of it all was earthed in my bodymind. The anger was deeply embedded, on top of my born angry persona. Pain, panic and *crazy* ruled my life. Yesterday was every day for hours, weeks, months and years. For such a long time, so many sorrowful memories, betrayals and abuses haunted me. Living in the present was unbearable. Envisioning a return to wholeness was nearly impossible.

Ultimately, the awakening I experienced with Lodie explained a great deal about the anger and angst that trademarked my life and held my Spirit hostage for over 40 years. Whatever anyone else may believe, I am clear that my first rebirthing experience was a shining example of the adage, "When the student is ready, the teacher will come."

This transformative session also allowed me to witness my healing intelligence at its best. Lodie and I did not have a specific treatment plan, just a healing intention and an openness to the mysteries of energy work. This experience would prove to be foundational to all that I would study in my energy medicine classes in the years to come.

To expound for a moment, I would later learn that one of the primary tenets in biodynamic craniosacral therapy is that "the treatment plan is inherent," meaning that healing wisdom resides within each of us. I call this inner wisdom that guides the self-healing process the three I's: Inherent Intelligent Intention.

Ironically, the illuminating experience with Lodie also reminded me of my mother's story about how I broke out in a rash the day after I was born. I say that I had an "allergic reaction" to being born. Mother went on to share with me that the remedy applied to my skin turned me blue. When I arrived home to be introduced to my siblings, I was received with gasps and disbelief and rejection. Nobody wanted a "blue baby" for a sister. That shed some light on my fears of coming out!

Let me say for the record that I may never know for sure where my fear of birth originated. On the surface, the potential for great suffering is surely enough to rock the earthly boat. For all I know, this fear programming started in another lifetime. What I am prone to consider relevant is that it was necessary to my Soul's incarnation of its highest version of itself and me as a victorious warrior. There had to be seemingly insurmountable obstacles to overcome. What greater conflict than to not want to be born, period!

I would spend the next 20 years seeking answers to this underlying challenge of the tenor of my birth. As always, I would find answers when I was not looking.

Mother Mary

A few years later in a craniosacral therapy class, I had my second rebirthing experience. The source of the unveiling was another practice session, only this time the session had a very specific intention—to palpate the third ventricle of the brain. I call this place, "the Holy of Holies" of the body. The Breath of Life, also known as Source energy or essence, does much of its magic in the third ventricle of the brain.

As was the class custom, we chose our partners before starting the session. We were always encouraged to find someone with whom we had not worked before, which was often quite intimidating.

Blessing of all blessings, I had the good fortune to be paired with the one lady in the class who embodied the feminine principle of motherhood. Mary was the mother of eight children and admired by everyone in the class for her enormous mothering heart. Mary's love for her family was palpable.

This was our first and the only time we worked together. As the session came into fullness, I shifted into a place of vividly shinning bright white light. I could feel the light glowing within my head as I sensed a sudden swoosh of energy coming through a lighted tunnel. It was "baby me" coming through that tunnel—an energetic birth canal. My eyes felt like spinning wheels. My whole body felt effortlessly illuminated. I was born again, and I knew it! Somehow I knew that I was cleansed at the Source of my being of birth trauma long held within my energy body.

This second rebirthing experience was even more powerful than the first. My awareness of my self within the cycle of birth went even deeper than before. Now I knew it was okay to be born. Layers of fear were forever cleansed from my body, mind and soul. Better yet, I witnessed the power of the healing white Light. I saw the face of God. I felt the call to go forth and heal with a peace beyond human understanding.

Miracle of miracles, when I got off the table I was walking on air. Yet I felt grounded and stable on my feet. Again, I knew something significant had occurred although I did not yet fully understand it.

An even more tangible reality set in later that evening when I went home to rest before the next day's class. My fibromyalgia pain level had dropped substantially throughout my body. I could sense a complete shift in my myofascial system. My vision was clearer and sharper. Healing energies permeated every cell of my body. I was deeply humbled and profoundly grateful to God.

Born angry?

My third rebirthing led me to the conclusion that I was born angry with a deep certainty that defied proof. Notwithstanding this empirical dilemma, my knowing self held the truth with abundant clarity. Once again Divine Intelligence smiled on me in a therapeutic environment. It is no surprise that I was once again engaged in an open discovery session with a close friend and colleague.

For over a decade, my craniosacral polarity therapist, Tom Langan, has been one of the gatekeepers of my quest for wellness and freedom from pain and panic. We met as students in a craniosacral therapy course with the Wellness Institute in 1998. During our years of study, we worked together only a couple of times—once when I needed a little extra grounding. When the course was over, my regular therapist was expecting a baby and was not available to continue our weekly sessions. Tom was available and accessible in the D.C. area. Our learning curve would ebb and flow through all the sessions and trainings we shared in the ensuing years.

While pursuing studies in aromatherapy in 2004, Tom "brought in" or channeled a healing protocol that he named, Re-imprinting. In the midst of a powerful soul excursion, he was gifted with this healing paradigm. As Tom's loyal guinea pig, I was among the first to experience the protocol in action. Another miracle was waiting for me in the cosmic energy field. Tom and I had many great experiments, miracles and mysteries under our belts. This one was the cherry on top!

Re-imprinting gave Tom and me specific access to the higher chakras of soul development in the energy anatomy. Stretching beyond the standard knowledge of the seven major chakras (the body's major energy centers), Tom journeyed up to the twelfth chakra. Situated above the crown chakra, "transpersonal" chakras, as he called them, were uncharted territory for us. Our experience of these higher chakras opened the door to stages of human development beyond the embryo. So we went looking for answers to unknown questions.

So what is a chakra? (Thought you would never ask!) *Chakra* is a Sanskrit word meaning spinning wheel or vortex. The seven continuously pulsating midline energy centers are aligned in an ascending column from the base of the spine to the top of the head. In brief, these chakras function as gateways through which subtle energy or vital force is distributed. Chakras transform the primary energy of the Breath of Life into the various qualities of the five universal elements—ether, air, fire, water and earth.

Six of the commonly identified chakras are located along the physical midline, near the coccyx, top of the sacrum, the solar plexus, at the heart, in the throat and in the center of the cranium. The sixth chakra in the center of the brain resides in the third ventricle and is often referred to as the "third eye" or the "seat of consciousness." The seventh or crown chakra resides slightly above the top of the head and is a point of unity consciousness.

To elevate this story just a bit more, the Re-imprinting protocol involved special chakra oils for each stage of the interrogatory healing process. A talented alchemist from France channeled the essential oil blends that we used. Tom and I included essential oils with much success in many bodywork sessions. Now the mysteries were overflowing in this new land of Re-imprinting. More important, it was Tom's creation. A new tool for expanding the healing process had been born.

You are probably saying, "Stop right here! Surely your interpretation is flawed. You and this guy had a thing going on!"

And, yes, we did have a really good client-practitioner relationship with a history of amazing results and progress with many modalities and resources. So we had many things going on. We worked with tuning forks, sublingual minerals, crystals, vibrational CDs, light therapy and on and on. It was our stock in trade to build a storehouse of resources. It was important to have an array of tools available to provide a diverse set of healing opportunities for clients and for our own self-healing journey.

In many of our sessions, we reduced pain, balanced chakras and realigned structure. We discharged the horrific trauma associated with Post Traumatic Stress Disorder (PTSD) that I suffered after the flood that nearly killed my daughter and me in 2001. We observed with awe the innate dynamic of what we call "autonomic yoga" emerge as the dance of energetic intelligence at its effortless best. Tom and I routinely lived in the land of Aha! and Wow!

So, yes, we had a thing going on! But it was not the kind of thing most people think about. As practitioners with integrity and everything to lose if we looked like idiots, Tom and I were very careful with our claims of attribution. The realm of anecdotal mysteries was both familiar and reliable in our estimation and in our experience. The standard measures of test-re-test reliability and statistical significance were far removed. Our training in energy medicine opened our hearts and minds to allowing the innate Intelligence to inform our work and our interpretations. We were comfortable with the new mythology that was emerging before our eyes in our work together.

The energy bodywork session that revealed this incredible idea of being born angry was in many ways no different than others Tom and I had learned from over the years. We were allowing an opportunity for discovery to manifest through chakra oils aligned with specific dimensions of the energy anatomy. We were following a well-established polarity therapy concept, which explores a step-down through the layers of the wireless anatomy, a hierarchical hologram. In brief, this concept describes the energetic development of the human bodymind coming into form from the dimensions of Soul and Spirit. This sacred calling beyond the veil was common ground for two adventurous polarity/craniosacral practitioners who had studied and practiced together for a number of years. So we were pioneers to the end.

From common ground, we were lifted to much higher ground as we worked through the re-imprinting protocol. Tom took me step by step into each upper level chakra with the intention to be informed by the Breath of Life at every portal.

I will be eternally grateful to my craniosacral therapy mentors who literally gave me the Breath of Life. I understand it both as a physiologic experience and a core principle in energy healing. More important, it is the union of body and spirit that I longed for.

The Breath of Life has many clinical interpretations, not to mention scriptural import. In brief, it is the *inherent life force* that orders all things in creation as well as the Source of all creation. In many ways, the Breath of Life is a complex idea to consider. At the same time that it is the primary, driving pulsation in the cerebrospinal fluid in the body, it is also the energetic expression of the cells and the connection of same to Source. I will say more about this essence of all life in the section of this book on therapies that worked for me.

Tom and I were accustomed to allowing the numerous expressions of the Breath of Life to inform our healing journey. The midline chakras were the perfect places to observe this force in action. Time and time again, we had explored the seven chakras during our training in energy medicine. The day of the Re-imprinting experience, we were stepping down through the veil of mysteries of conception and preconception held in the higher chakras.

When I came into a passage through the divine feminine energy field, the ninth chakra, I sensed an erratic and fitful disturbance in the field. All at once I knew that my conception was imprinted with friction and fearful tension. In that moment, I understood that perhaps my parents were not in harmony. Maybe a few hurtful words were exchanged earlier that day. I will never know for certain. For whatever reason, I had a profoundly soul-stirring epiphany. I shouted out to Tom, "Aha, I was born angry! Is it possible I was born angry?"

Tom was as awestruck as I as we pondered this astonishing possibility.

What could this mind-boggling idea—"born angry"—really mean? Was I conceived in some momentary field of anger to fulfill my soul's choosing? Is that why I was sick at birth and for another lifetime? Is that why I co-created fibromyalgia? Is that why I have panic disorder and the mission of healing in this lifetime and in this book? So many questions flooded my consciousness.

As they say, the damage was done. My incarnated soul was fractured at conception. Again, what an idea! What a confusing soul's choice. Or was I just delusional in that moment with Tom searching for answers in all the wrong places? I really don't need to know the answer to the last question. All the questions are sufficient to my purposes in inviting the potential for all possibilities.

Re-imprinting settled the score for all time. Another new beginning was born in my soul. A new lightness filled my Spirit. Now I knew for sure, there were answers beyond the horizon. Something else happened in the energetic time line of my birth. I had to look in order to see. I felt my preconceived self beyond the view of my cells. My pioneer spirit reached nirvana that day!

I had walked with anger that was larger than life for almost all of my life before rebirthing or Re-imprinting came into the equation. I was always prone to some form of internalized sadness, even as a young child. It is comforting to understand why, even if the causes dwell in the land of mystery. I am grateful for the divine opportunity to know my soul stories as instruments of transformation and healing grace.

To learn more about the transformative power of Re-imprinting, log on to www.setherapies.org. The website, which calls this healing treatment, Energetic Re-Imprinting or ERI, gives further examples of successful applications of this health-building work.

Boot Camp for the Soul

So just when I thought I had been to the mountaintop of rebirthing, I learned that there were yet higher peaks to climb. The "born angry" saga called forth what I call, "My greatest story ever told."

It was another ordinary day in the summer of 2013 or so I thought. Thu-Hien Poma of Adonai, eclectic High Priestess of energy healing, was awed by the depths of the soul journey we experienced on what became a most memorable day. Again I lingered in suspended animation as another transfiguring soul secret unraveled its invisible code.

Our remote healing session came quite by accident or perhaps by synchronicity. I was following through with a few referrals when I felt the nudge to schedule a telephone session with Thu-Hien. I was a bit surprised by my inclination for yet another session. I had just had a session in July that was very powerful. Nonetheless, I followed my intuitive call and waited for her call.

As our usual way of "settling in" to begin a session, she offered an opening prayer. We exchanged a few updates and reflections on our last healing session. I was always amazed by her presence in my soul life. I proceeded to unload my latest burdens and challenges.

Her deepening breaths were audible through the phone lines as she reached for answers to my burning questions. The most pressing and perplexing question came up often: "Why so many betrayals?"

Thu-Hien's answer to the question of betrayals would become the greatest story ever told in my life, in my recollection. I had heard many, many stories both highly plausible and some just downright nonsensical. This soul story had the ring of truth from someone with a very rare and unique connection to the multidimensional world of Spirit.

"Boot Camp for the Soul," she called it.

"You chose it!" Thu-Hien replied when I needed more of a reason to understand what she meant. "You asked for the darkest thing you could get in this lifetime," the beautiful young healer told me, "so you could look out on the world as a victorious warrior not as a wounded, defeated person."

She added that, in addition to the challenge of this lifetime, I also was given the strength to overcome.

Like a character in a video game, I wanted the baddest opponent so I could have the most tremendous soul growth. Essentially, I had asked to be victorious in defeating the devil. So the devil was playing a game with me.

Upon further reflection on this invitation to the devil business, I asked, "Who does that?"

The response "You do!" did not comfort my Spirit. It was not easy to hear that I had chosen to dance with the ultimate betrayer seeking to win my soul's glory.

As we journeyed together farther into my shadows, it became apparent that betrayal was my greatest test of personal fortitude. Simply put, betrayal was my gauntlet of faith and hope. It was my signature form of self-sabotage. What others did to me, I then did to myself, claiming the "devil made me do it."

For sure I must be a bad girl! So many others seemed to think so. So I "brought in" a little insurance at birth to be assured of a life filled with traumatizing relationships.

I listened intently to Thu-Hien "receive" this incredible story through channels unknown to me. Suddenly, I burst into tears. The tremendous weight of years spent wondering why I was so misunderstood, bullied and humiliated was lifted from my shoulders. In a moment's notice, the broader view of my lifetime of turmoil, tragedies and traumas became clearer. This was not a case of random selection.

Going deeper and deeper, she continued, "You brought it in with you at birth. Babies are not born innocent, you know."

I began to well up again. I relived those years of agony, desperate to find meaning and purpose.

To Thu-Hein, I kept saying, "It makes so much sense. It explains a lot!"

As I absorbed the impact of Thu-Hein's commentary, words

lost their import for a bit. My Spirit was reeling with confusion about my birth. I had never heard anything so sensational in all my life! The revelations she shared took on dimensions that shook me to the core. I was a little intimidated by the direction the story could be taking. Somehow I knew this was a journey that would change my life forever.

So now I needed to know much more about this "boot camp for the soul." Certainly, there was more to the story. What *it* was she talking about? What could have the power to cast my Soul into a pit of betrayals? How could this be a force for good? How could this yield a warrior?

Myriad questions loomed in the atmosphere of my imagination while I listened to the rest of the sordid details unfold. In all honesty, the grand drama sounded like something the "black sheep" would do. I must confess, it made me cringe.

Even the modern day metaphysics I proclaim so loudly and often did not prepare me for this macabre tale about my Soul's choices. Enlightenment was not so warm and fuzzy in light of these developments.

The *it* that I brought into this life was a dark, negative, lower vibration entity—feminine, of course—with a sinister countenance whose sole mission was to destroy me and my life. This entity had traveled with me through many lifetimes. It was as though I was always carrying an enemy with me that did not want me to succeed. Betrayal was one of her Medusa-like modus operandi, by any means possible. Thu-Hien called the entity a "shock-Jack."

For the sake of balance, it is fair to say that this entity was not all bad or all negative. She represented my haunting enemy within. Ironically, she was also quite useful in recognizing my "green-eyed" adversaries and keeping them at bay.

This entity may have been the reason that I was able to shake off the bully who sent me hate mail every day in the fifth grade.

Whenever I stood up to recite my times tables—effortlessly I might add—she was somewhere slouching in her chair. No matter how many threatening notes she wrote saying, "I am going to best you," it was never going to happen. It never did! And she was not very big so she was not going to jump me. I was safe, thanks to the "dark one" who fought alongside me. No contest. No competition. Every grading period, I was still #1. And I could spell!

I never thought of myself as competitive until this session with Thu-Hien. I still don't! Now I understand why I had to have a fierce competitor living within me to handle the battlefield moments.

Undermining my relationship with my mother was high on the list of chicanery and mischief perpetrated by this internal nemesis. She brought grief to my mother through me, making her feel helpless with me, Thu-Hien explained as she unearthed more of the shocking story. I suppose my "Daddy's-girl" attributes made the mother-daughter conflict easy to penetrate and agitate. As I think about it, most of my primary relationships hit a stone wall at some point with rare exception.

As the healing session continued, the details got eerier and crisper as High Priestess Thu-Hien called forth messages from unknown worlds—at least unknown to me. Again, I replied, "It makes so much sense. It explains a lot!"

When I recovered from the emotional overwhelm of such a fantastical soul story, I recognized the potency of such a revelation as "super-thrive" fertilizing my way ahead. The fact that there was an explanation for the puzzling complexities of this lifetime was like jet propulsion to my forward progress. What next?

Then came the true miracle in action! The entity was ready to be removed from my energy field by remote healing practices. The very act of calling her out had diminished her *force majeure* and had opened the door for her banishment from my life. Thu-Hien counseled, "You must thank your opponent. The game is over!"

The soul-to-soul connection between the priestess and me would now set forth the design of its grandest story yet. "How do I get rid of it?" I asked. Fortunately, I was working with a naturally gifted practitioner who had lifetimes of angelic resonance and was skilled at distance healing. Thu-Hein conducts seminars and healing sessions on many international stages and in the rain forests and mountains of faraway places.

After a productive chakra-clearing exercise, I was instructed to lie down on my treatment table and allow Thu-Hien to do the additional cleansing work from her remote location. This would require deep surrender. She told me I would probably go to sleep. And I did. But before I slept, I could feel the work as if she were there in the room with me like any other energy worker.

This was one of the few times in my 20-plus years receiving energy work sessions that I fell into such a deep repose. Other therapists often chastised me for not falling asleep during bodywork sessions. I always wanted to stay awake and witness the miracles and the mystery of the movements of energy medicine treatments. I was often too much in my head. My passion to learn and understand the work was so strong I needed to be the constant observer. The researcher in me was always collecting and analyzing incoming data.

The energy work was always effective in spite of my mental tendencies. But this session with Thu-Hien was extraordinary. Deep rest both during and after the treatment was essential to its full and complete success.

Upon awakening from the healing sleep an hour later, I was filled with humility and gratitude. I *knew* something miraculous had happened. The days that followed were full of light and inspiration. A certain sense of ease was palpable in my Spirit. My Soul accepted her diploma and marched forward into a greater mystery.

I suppose that I will need a little time to know for sure if this demonic entity is still bringing me grief and undermining my joy.

For the most part, I believe that outing her at least diminished her power over me. Perhaps, the relief I have come to feel from freeing her will need periodic reinforcements. I am okay with any follow-up that may be required to keep her away. I am so ready to graduate from Boot Camp!

This monumental healing event took place just eight days after my 65th birthday. As I iterated earlier, this particular session with Thu-Hien was not planned but called to order by a higher power. I should have known it would be big!

To learn more about Thu-Hien and her remarkable healing work, logon to www.thuhien.org.

Skeptics will say I am crazy for sure for telling these stories. Many will deny that anything in this chapter ever happened outside of my convoluted imagination. Some friends and family will say, "I told you so! She is a goner! Get her some real help, quick! I told you, she is crazy!"

I say, "Thank you" to my whole self for recognizing that the pathway to healing holds treasures we cannot always measure or explain in ordinary or scientific terms. Mystery is the miracle that leads to our own special truth. Each of us has unique gifts and a unique soul truth for which we are called to be responsible stewards. I call this soul phenomenon, *gifts with responsibilities.*

For me, my sacred contract with healing is one of these gifts. Sharing my miraculous journey is my responsibility as a storyteller and a victorious warrior. Telling the world how I learned to seek the blessing in every challenge and to hold the intention of rising above all adversity is the mission that matters. This author's path is perhaps my most remarkable gift in 2014 and my most sacred responsibility. Whether I am writing a poem, crafting this narrative or mirroring the path to a fellow soul seeker, I have a clear and conscious call to inspire and encourage others to heal. I am honored to *know* this calling and recognize it.

Soul work has been around for eons. Shamans and soul astrologers have traveled around the world bringing relief to weary and confused Earth dwellers for centuries. I am both humbled and honored to be enlightened by the healing gifts of a powerful few. Thank you, Lodie, Tom, Mother Mary and Thu-Hien for being my Soul guides.

So, yes, I can accept that my birth energy was confounded by a negative charge of soul energy. The "dark side" was my greatest challenge, my greatest teacher and my greatest story ever told.

In my daily life in 2014, I think of this remarkable arising from the challenges of boot camp as an invitation to know my own soul's polarity. This dance with the devil was a necessary part of my spiritual growth. Each healing cycle brought me closer and closer to a quality of living imbued with balance, harmony and unity with God.

I purged negative self-talk from my consciousness. With much concerted effort, I quieted the default "committee" in my head leading me astray—subconsciously. Thanks to the writings of Iyanla Vanzant, I "re-languaged" my thoughts and the words that I let flow from my mouth. This transformative process changed my heart in wondrous ways! Beneath the layers of self-hatred, I found the self-love that was waiting to heal my angry soul. I learned the truth that set me free forever: *Love Is the Answer*.

I imagine there are many readers of this book who can lay claim to a similar experience of transformation without such a high drama narrative. I invite you to tell your story.

It would take the better part of two decades to purge my anger, make amends and restore peace to my weary countenance. So the idea of *Boot Camp for the Soul* is the perfect metaphor for my earthly mission so far. Paradoxically, the anger with which I was born was, by far, one of my most compelling healers. Unveiling and understanding its power over my joy led to my empowerment as a self-healer.

The gift of forgiveness was worth the wait. It is my most loving endowment.

And so the *Already Angry* poem moves to the Light and concludes:

So I'll forgive you,
If you'll forgive me.
And turn already angry
Into forever free!

So while we are on the subject, where is your anger meter? High? Low? Medium? Off the Chart? Your Soul might be glad you asked!

A new chapter is beginning in 2014. We will see where it goes! Stay tuned!

CHAPTER 3

Dis-eases and Diagnoses

F ROM *A PARADOX*—POEM BY JUSTPAULA:

My illness taught me
To be well,
Even though I had to pass through hell.

My list of diagnoses is pretty maddening all by itself. But I learned from each one of them. At least the symptoms I experienced finally had names and identities. In my mind, nothing could be so obviously wrong to me and yet observable to no one else.

It took several highly qualified physicians to name all my diseases, one-by-one as they emerged. Soon there was a complete package of disharmonies that represented parts of my fractured body and soul. I was categorically and undeniably disabled and unable to perform my life skills and work skills with any semblance of normalcy, much less frequency.

By the end of my gradual deterioration, I could barely raise my arms and hands to wash my shoulder-length hair that was now a necessity to keep my neck warm. I was in excruciating pain 24/7 when I wasn't drugged or exhausted into sleep filled with panicky dreams and night sweats. There was a bowl of meds at my bedside, and the highlight of my day was a lavender shower, if I could make it to the bathroom and stand up long enough to enjoy it.

Pain: Myofascial Trigger-Point Disorder

The physical pain came first. One spring day, I was in my private office at work when I got a severe chill from the cold air blowing through the overhead air conditioning vent.

I am certain that day started much like any other. I drove to work, parked my car and settled into my assignments like I did every other day.

I had felt some unexplained leg pain during the autumn prior to this defining day in March. But this time, the pain was in my neck and left shoulder. It became severe very quickly as I continued to sit under the chilling AC in my office. In three days, I was leaving work early barely able to carry my briefcase in my left hand. By the time I arrived home, I was squatting, unable to walk properly due to the pain in my left side.

Little did I know that these three days would lead to a cascading stream of discomforts and disorders that would not only change my life as I knew it but also take me down to the depths of despair before my fall was complete. My future was cast!

Of course, I sought medical attention. However, there was no simple explanation for what was happening to me. There was no pain in my legs at the time or, at least, none I could perceive. The air conditioning problem was even more puzzling than the pain.

So for six months, from March to September, I went in and out of my office with intermittent pain until, one day in September, the cumulative impact rendered me in pain 24/7. It was on September 13, 1988, that I was referred to Dr. Michael Reynolds and the two diagnoses were born. My pain had a name and my experience with AC was validated.

After myriad preliminary diagnoses, i.e., bursitis, possible rheumatoid arthritis, landing in the capable hands of Dr. Reynolds was truly a blessing. Dr. Reynolds would be my first medical champion! I won't even allow myself thoughts about what would have happened to me if it were not for his expertise and faith in my case.

Dr. Reynolds was clear that what I was suffering from was a rarely diagnosed syndrome known as myofascial trigger-point disorder (MTPD). I had never heard of it before. This group of words would define my self-concept for many years to come. The name would soon fade away to a more popularized one-word interpretation. But that comes later. The moment would live on forever. In an instant, finding a name and an expert gave me fleeting feelings of sanity. I could finally proclaim that I was not imagining the pain or just plain ol' crazy.

My public was not impressed. To friends and most family members, it sounded like a lot of gobbledy-gook. The words did not communicate at all the pain and disability of the disorder. And, what is a disorder, for goodness sake? What are "trigger-points"? What is fascia? Why is it so painful?

What I needed to know was that these were the easy questions. Many, many more elusive unknowns would arise and taunt my existence for years to come. The invisibility of their presence was the most mystifying battle with my diagnoses. There was little to quantify to the novice observer. Even the experts were baffled by the pain patterns and fluctuations, the referred and unexplainable pain.

Dr. Reynolds was one of the most qualified specialists in the country treating the unfamiliar malady with the very specific name. It was no accident, this choice by the wondrous Universe of a highly skilled physician for me to work with. Finding a master healer was also the first rung on my ladder of spiritual growth, the first seed of healing. I would learn amazing things from Dr. Reynolds that would shape the course of my healing process. But I am getting ahead of myself.

Cold sensitivity

It seems like a reasonable plan to describe the chronology of my diseases in one fell swoop. So here goes: After myofascial trigger-point disorder, came cold-sensitivity. Now I was really in trouble. The latter was even more innocuous than the pain. But, fortunately for me, both my wonderful physicians, Drs. Adams and Reynolds, were familiar with the potential effects of cold temperatures on muscle discomfort. They were at least accepting of the idea that the air conditioning was indeed causing symptoms to increase, resulting in undue stress.

The doctors were the only ones who believed this physical stress was happening to me. Most people, not the least of all, my superiors at work, were skeptical at best and argumentative and rude to me at their worst.

I did not understand the reaction to the AC either. I just knew that when I got to work and sat under the extreme cold that was blowing from above my head onto my shoulders, I hurt worse. What I did not know then was that the AC from another office where repairs were being conducted had redirected the flow with greater intensity into my vent—or so I was told later.

Now, the first question I am always asked when I tell this story is "why didn't you get a heater?" The second thing most inquiring minds want to know is, "Did you report this to the authorities?" I usually take a breath and then offer the following explanations.

First, the authorities would not approve my having a heater and threatened to discipline me if I brought one of my own. After I fought this response for a time, my supervisor brought me a defective heater that I did not use for fear of worse reprisals.

But mostly, they would not help me because they did not believe me. It did not seem to matter how many times Dr. Adams wrote, "avoid cold temperatures" on my medical slip. The supervisors were not convinced that I was in any peril. Surely, I was acting out. I am a woman, and, well their attitude was typically misogynistic: "You know how women do."

In their defense, I might not have believed someone like me, either. I suspect that I would have believed their doctors though or at least attempted to meet the person halfway. Most of us would be better off without such narrow thinking. In this life, all things are possible with or without God. However, that is off the subject. Thinking *outside the box* was not popular in the late '80s and early '90s.

I got very little sympathy. No one wanted to help me. The unfamiliarity of my dilemma and closed minds were too pervasive. So I didn't get a heater for many reasons. It just wasn't that simple. But thanks for asking and, in some cases, thanks for caring. Some people, I learned, really do care and just don't know what to say.

My outward appearance was just not very believable! No one who looked as successful as I did, with my pedigree and background and other demographics, and, I guess, as well spoken and determined could be suffering as much as I claimed to be. Surely, I just needed to get over myself! I did not look sick!

Cold-sensitivity, what a farce! Air conditioning could never be the enemy. And there was no real precedent for what I was describing. Imagine a smart girl like me coming up with such a story. What was I thinking? I wasn't! I was suffering for real, it was just that the most influential people in my life didn't believe me.

Depression

It would be several years later before all the emotional layers of my disease would be diagnosed. The more I suffered physical pain and personal torment, the more my spirit cried and cried and fell into the abyss. I was diagnosed with major depression. This was not surprising. At least, it was familiar.

But depression was still a taboo subject for the most part. Depression ran in my family. I had this diagnosis in my early twenties. If you had it you did not talk about it, yet another taboo subject. Most people just wanted me to "get over it"(there's that phrase again) and go back to my normal self. Depression was considered more or less an inconvenience or a nuisance, not the debilitating life-altering condition that it really is.

There were new prescription medications for depression when I was in my early twenties in the '70s. I did well with short-term trials of Elavil and Triavil and seemed to return to normal back then. I wonder about that now. I took these meds with no counseling to support the healing process. In hindsight, I realize that healing couldn't occur without counseling and other healing modalities. I think I merely went into remission for a time.

Until the later diagnosis of depression was made, I was mainly on a cocktail of Darvocet for pain and Ativan for anxiety four times a day. Sometimes, I took just one or the other drug. Both were reasonably effective but, sometimes, neither worked. Over time they became less effective for pain, in particular. Some doctors even claimed that they were contraindicated.

Then came the anti-inflammatory meds, naproxen et al. Yuk! Predictably, this led to the need for digestive coating agents to protect and correct my tortured stomach lining, Zantac (when you needed a Rx for it). My extensive pharmacological array would not be complete without the antidepressants Paxil, Prozac, Zoloft, etc. When one didn't work, I was given another. Sometimes I was instructed to take two or more at a time. Next came the sleep aids, including Stadol (a general anesthesia), which cost $80 for a one-ounce bottle. This potent drug led to my date with detox after realizing I was extremely overmedicated and looming close to an overdose.

The realization that I needed a general anesthesia to go to sleep was more than my Spirit could handle.

"Surely, this will kill you," she cried out.

I would eventually realize that the intense meds had to go. It took ten years, but I finally got there. So with the diagnosis of depression came my descent into pharmaceutical toxicity.

Maybe that is why I thought I was going to die when I was having panic attacks. I always wondered why I would have that particular thought. Maybe my mind was trying to tell me something that I just now realized as I was writing this. I can see now how this realization could be defining. That is, there exists the possibility that some intense knowing that I was systematically poisoning myself could potentially make me think I was a goner.

I remember well the day that I figured out that I was killing myself, playing Russian roulette with medications. It was a breakthrough moment! The story is told in Chapter 8—stay tuned!

Panic disorder

So my diagnoses to that point included myofascial trigger-point disorder, cold sensitivity and major depression exacerbated by poor digestion, constipation, insomnia and expanding pain patterns. After intermittent bouts with Restless Leg Syndrome and teeth grinding, I had another defining day when I added the diagnosis of panic disorder.

I can still remember sitting in bed, reading the Bible. I really did not read scripture very often in those days. I was recovering from my latest injury at work and trying to comfort myself when, all of a sudden, I could not breathe. My heart started beating out of control. I jerked away so hard that the Bible flew from my hands onto the floor.

Sylver took me to the emergency room where I was hospitalized and sedated. I was probably angry about whatever situation had set me back. It was an all too frequent occurrence.

So there I was, afraid of everything, what I later discovered was my primary panic attack mode. There I lay in Howard University Hospital waiting for my system, whatever that means, to calm down and return to normal.

Well, I had a new normal. It was already not working for me. I struggled to regain control. Five days later, I was sent home to rest some more and recover my normalcy and return to function. In other words, no one knew what to do with a panic attack patient any more than they knew how to make some sense out of "cold sensitivity."

The longer my voyage continued, the cloudier the skies became. One pirate after another came to conquer any clarity I might begin to find. As soon as I understood one diagnosis, another appeared, more confusing than the one before it.

So my laundry list at that point in the early '90s included myofascial trigger-point disorder, cold sensitivity, depression and panic attacks.

My hospital visit proved providential. I was taken off my job and sent to a full-time pain clinic. I was completely disabled and suffering severe emotional imbalance tantamount to a major and complete nervous breakdown with all physical parts following suit.

Another key variable in this equation that has not been addressed yet is the path of the pain. Pain that began in my left shoulder and neck and spread quickly to my back on my left side would, over the first three years, encompass my entire body. Every time I passed through a layer of pain therapeutically, there was yet another pain pattern in yet another muscle. The fact that I got worse for years still haunts me.

The pain clinic was another empowering experience that ended badly. There was a special lady there whose determination to help me matched my determination to get better. She studied my case at night and tried new therapies that she was learning in addition to the ones prescribed by the doctors. She was enthusiastic and brave and even allotted more time for me, which she had to defend before the powers that be allowed it. She also led my physical therapy exercise routine. It was in this clinic that I first used an exercise ball to regain my balance. (It is now one of my favorite things!)

I was a good student. For six months, she led and I followed precisely. I am certain that we inspired each other.

I lived in a hotel and went home on the weekends, primarily to sing in church, another key component of my medical, emotional and spiritual regimen.

I was married at the time, so my husband drove me back and forth every week. Fortunately, he liked to drive. But I don't think he would appreciate for the long-term all that was required for my healing to take root. I don't fault him for that either. I was struggling with no end in sight for months and years. Most people who meet me now have no understanding of the place I came from. That is good and bad and perhaps another reason that I write. It is important that my stories are not forgotten. The past is my prologue. The present is derivative.

I did not acquire any new diagnoses in this clinic. I just struggled with the already existing ones and endured some badly administered trigger-point injections. The latter would ultimately end my therapeutic endeavors at the clinic.

The primary physician who gave the painful excuses for treatment was perhaps the worst possible practitioner with the injection protocol. He was also the head of the clinic. Too often, he poked and prodded until he drew blood, tears and rage.

One fateful day he went too far with the needle and sent me reeling into a rage-filled panic attack that sent me running out of the clinic. Fortunately for me, my daughter and husband were waiting in the car in front of the clinic and could rescue me post haste. Fortunately for them, I was still rational enough to ensure that we left that place rapidly before one of us resorted to violence.

I had been in constant conflict with this particular clinic doctor for the six months I was being treated there. We argued about sit-ups and injection sites and emotional flare-ups week in and week out. It was perhaps one of the worst falls that I took through the 15-year rehabilitative journey. Once again, I was completely reinjured by the time I left after six months of intensive therapy.

I was in screaming pain and a basket case because I could not communicate with my doctor. From that moment on, I would add to my list of dis-eases, what I labeled, "doctor-phobia." All doctors were suspect, except for Drs. Adams and Reynolds. These medical giants were my rocks of Gibraltar through all of this, writing one referral after another as my condition went up and down and up and down. I never counted the times. Perhaps when I am finished with this writing, I will have a close count of the big ones.

When the breakdown in the pain clinic occurred, I had been almost fully restored to physical functioning. Thanks to my devoted and diligent physical therapist, I could walk without a cane. I could take dance classes again. I was still on pain meds, but they were much more effective. I had an excellent exercise regimen. I had faithfully worked out twice a day, six days a week for six months. This included swimming once a day, physical therapy six days a week with my gifted therapist plus regular counseling.

The counseling services at the clinic were not very effective. As a matter of fact, with one exception, I learned only to hate talk therapists. Like the doctor, the therapists argued with me about why I was reacting as I was rather than helping me to change my behavior. I just needed to "get over it" and "behave myself" and "not act out." I'd heard that before! I was prone to do all of that and more when the needle gave more pain than pain relief.

My doctor's punishment became an order to "drop and do 20" when I acted out. I learned to use this insult to my advantage even though it was excruciatingly painful getting started. Push-ups became my friend for a while and really helped to strengthen my arms.

You see, I refused to be punished. It was an innate talent, I think, along with the anger.

One of my few early childhood memories involves playing in the punishment chair in the front hall of our enormous house on Montague Street in Charleston. I would climb all around the chair to pretend that I was not being punished, but rather having fun in a contained space. Yes, I was a little strange from the beginning. At least, I reconciled punishment at some level.

In any case, I left the clinic, in some ways, more disabled than when I started. The healers' betrayal was the ultimate blow. I was once again at rock bottom and starting over with a new set of therapies in my viewfinder.

I was also meandering through the bureaucratic maze of medical leave and grappling with the cost of all this therapy and who would pay for it at the same time all of these events were taking place. So I had, as my church friend used to say, "Trouble on every side." I was, you know, just damned.

I wasn't able to hold onto anything I tried for very long, in spite of all the miracles and healings that had begun. There was always some drama, medical or otherwise, that stole my spirit and reduced me to physical rubble.

Dysthymia

Then there was pain clinic number two, preceded by one of my most memorable psychiatrists, who would give me my next diagnosis. Dysthymia, he called it: It means chronic sadness.

Now how about that? There is a medical name for "crying all the time."

This new diagnosis led me to the idea of layers. I am grateful for that lesson. The onion metaphor is very applicable to the dis-ease called fibromyalgia. I truly was crying all the time, even when there was nothing truly significant to cry about. This continuum of tears might have been normal for some other fair lady, but crying had never been my game.

As a child, I was taught not to cry, so it just didn't come easily after all those years of conditioning. Plus, I already had an extra layer of crying from the depression. But this crying was different. These tears expressed the sadness that had gone deeper and deeper into my soul with each setback. I was blindsided frequently by so many activating trigger events.

Dysthymia was different from depression. The associated crying spells were distinctive and clear when they came. Sometimes I cried endlessly on the heels of a depressive bout as I came through the channels of my spirit.

I soon learned that my cousin (on my mother's side) had the same diagnosis. It was very comforting to be validated so close to home. She was also someone that I could talk to.

I guess I always knew I had these tears inside me. My Spirit cried and cried and cried and cried and cried. Then I stopped crying and just became sad. All the time, I just felt sad—sad for my health, sad for my life and sad for everything around me.

No tears for Peepeye

I am thinking this could be a good place for my "Peepeye" story. The crying disorder I am describing here will make more sense and have greater context. It is a sunny tale of childhood grace.

There would be no tears for little "Peepeye." Punishment would always be deeply held and invisible to the naked eye. Perhaps this is the reason I was always "squinting" or "peeping." Maybe this is why my mother began calling me "Peepeye."

My guess today is that I really had a vision problem. I was wearing glasses by the fifth grade. I imagine I had impaired vision much earlier than was diagnosed. Or maybe I was just a quirky little kid.

In any case, early in my childhood, I learned not to cry. It was part of the punishment tradition in my family. "You better not cry," was law. Most of the time I could not help but cry. But the idea of this oppressive rule ran deep. "Better not cry" was the ultimate insult to whatever caused the injury.

The "no cry rule" did not seem to explain why I seemed never to respond to traditional punishment. I guess my own self-punishment outranked my external influences. This idea of the enemy within is a major part of the underlying story that has so many causal relationships to the person I became later in life.

Parental punishment took many forms depending on the infraction and its severity. Many times I would be commanded to sit in the chair in the hall—usually by my mother. The command would most assuredly include the caveat, "Stay there until I tell you to get up. And be quiet!"

The expectation was that being asked to sit silently in one place for hours would make a small child very unhappy. I can still picture my four-year old, pleasingly plump self in the big hall chair, as if it were yesterday. I can still visualize myself climbing around the legs and seat of the chair, ostensibly, "on punishment."

I consider it an awesome gift of earliest childhood development that I did not really understand the concept of punishment. I dare say I did not fully understand at that tender age why I was sitting in the chair for hours. For sure, this tendency for innocence is a form of protection for small children.

As I think about it now in 2014, sitting in silence was not

painful in the classical sense. It was nothing like the humiliation of getting a spanking. If I had any talent for comparisons then, which I doubt, the hall chair was the light punishment for sure.

Somehow there was no rule that said I had to sit still. Thank goodness for that! It would be 50-some years before I would find the presence of the stillness as the center of my peace.

So punishment with flexible rules became a metaphor and opportunity for exploration to the clever toddler. A little nimble choreography went a long way. After all, I was in my first dance recital at the age of four.

I climbed around and through and in and out of all the places and spaces the chair could provide. I imagine it was fun in the present moment and even a little confusing. Nonetheless, sitting in the hall on punishment was an adult idea. Sitting in the hall in the chair in my child's mind went something like, "Oh, OK, Mommy. It's that chair thing again!"

The consternation on my mother's face probably did not warm my heart. She checked in periodically to witness the suffering. The frequency of chair-sitting punishment was probably more than I would prefer to own. I believe the opportunity for spiritual growth was embedded in the experience.

My mother said that I always managed to entertain myself when she punished me in this manner. I am sure I was often caught in the midst of my gymnastic genius. I doubt that I had any concept of entertainment. It is more plausible to me that "life was entertainment" at age four.

My mother's quest for "signs of pain" was exaggerated by whatever event put me in the hall chair in the first place. Most parents want punishment to be something you can feel. My mother was no exception.

In many ways, I was no exception either. I was probably not the first preschooler to figure out how to make the best of a bad situation while on punishment. I would say now that this reaction was my best version of being an optimist. Hooray for Peepeye! The pessimism would come much later. I am grateful for this story to remind me of a time when I had a hopeful spirit. No tears were needed. Little Peepeye was all over it, quite literally!

The Peepeye story makes me smile in the midst of recalling the tears dysthymia brought to my eyes. This dis-ease of chronic sadness was yet another layer of my tortured psyche. This fifth dimension was another safe place for my broken spirit to hang out. I was relieved when I learned there was a name for what I was feeling. I cried about that too.

The idea of sadness was not nearly as threatening as the idea of panic. So dysthymia was a softer mental and emotional condition in my dis-ease lexicon. It was treatable and not especially life threatening. There is that phrase again. Somehow, I am offended by the idea that any one soul could judge what indeed poses a threat to another solitary soul. Maybe it would be an abusive father for you, maybe it's a mother who never said, "I love you," maybe a disabled sibling for someone else.

Each person responds individually to the same and different stimuli. It is not for me to say how you should define what happens to you. My interpretation of the same experience is in all probability different from yours.

The treatment plan for the diagnosis of dysthymia is another nightmarish story, ending with an Rx for bipolar disorder and schizophrenia. I think this doctor went out on a limb with the drugs. But I guess he was doing as he was taught and as he believed.

Stadol, the general anesthesia prescribed for sleep disturbance, was the crowning glory and ultimately became a powerful teacher, as you will learn more about in Chapter 8. Stadol was prescribed in addition to the antidepressants and, at the same time, in combination with my favorites, Darvocet and Ativan. The anti-inflammatories and stomach coaters were also included in the regimen. I would take four doses of eight to ten meds depending on the day and the level of discomfort or crazy. It is a miracle that I did not die from an overdose!

Just prior to the dysthymia doctor, I had a three-month stint at another pain clinic at a famous hospital. My case would once again be assigned to the director of the clinic. It was yet another treatment plan that ended badly. Several months of no-progress later, as it relates to the pain doctor, I left on the heels of another panic attack brought on by another social worker telling me to "Get over it."

But destiny always had some powerful experience in store in these places. There was always one individual who made a significant difference in my healing process, no matter where I ended up.

At that hospital, I learned about a new medical discipline called psychometry when I was referred to a psychometrist for biofeedback training for panic disorder.

My frequent panic attacks worsened the physical pain, sometimes for weeks. Biofeedback proved to be very effective and also taught me progressive muscle relaxation, a skill that I use to this day.

Although this training was not so easy to grasp either, I persevered and made great progress in understanding my complaint and how to control it through breathing. Breathwork would be one of my most useful and valued learnings for a lifetime. It is also the reason, in great measure, why I sing and why I wrote this book. The breath is one of our greatest God-given resources. Most of us take breathing for granted. We fail to use it for therapeutic results, when it is such a powerful healing tool.

What a shame! I hope this book changes this fact, if nothing more. I have used several types of breathing exercises to manage both pain and anxiety with incredible results. I think I read somewhere recently that Dr. Andrew Weil gives all his patients breathing exercises. Hallelu!

Dissociation

So now my list includes myofascial trigger-point disorder, panic attacks, cold sensitivity, depression, dysthymia, pharmaceutical toxicity, and manifesting agoraphobia (fear of open spaces) and doctor-phobia. Next on the laundry list were dissociative tendencies that came to light on the polarity therapy table with my beloved Charmaine.

By that time, I was at the height of crazy and out-to-lunch. The die was cast and yesterday became today and tomorrow was around the bend of insanity. The family of medical layers was complete, or at least I hoped it was.

Disintegration of a human soul was systematically discharged with the help of well-meaning professionals. The pain and disability were still raging. I imagine I was angry about a lot of things by that time. I imagine that I found it almost impossible not to be angry about everything.

Born angry began to fall in line with all the other injustices and fated events. I have only scratched the surface of this story and shared the highlights, giving you my own personal landmarks. The lessons are what mattered and led to my discovery of the things that worked for me. This storytelling gives context and perspective to the Truth that was unearthed and the Self-Love that was victorious in the final analysis. At least, this is what I believe 25 years later.

So how did I get to the polarity table?

One of my favorite things gets all the credit. Dancing was always one of my most fulfilling enterprises, as I have already shared more than once. I was in my first dance recital at the age of four and took classes throughout my childhood and high school years. While my daughter was growing up, I took dance lessons across the hall from her classes. In my late teens, I started a young beginner dance troupe at the college where I grew up. In my late twenties, I taught a class in "dancercise" from one of our apartment living rooms in College Park, Maryland.

For many years, I attended dance conferences with my dance buddy, Katherine James. She and I were students of Washington, D.C.–based dance teacher, Linda Verrill. We performed in frequent recitals for fun.

Katherine was an excellent role model for me. In all our years of dancing together, I never knew her age. She was faithful to the idea that "women don't tell" their age, ever. I respected her position. I suspect that she was 15 to 20 years older than I when I was in my early thirties. She carried herself with a youthful exuberance and fashionable style that impacted my own personal style statement, I am certain.

I was Sylver's first dance teacher when she was two and a half. It was the best babysitting idea that I ever invented. A faculty member at Voorhees, asked me to teach dance to the campus kids. It seemed like a plausible idea because my dance teacher, Linda DeVane, always told me that I should teach dance. She often called upon me to assist her to teach difficult steps. This was quite an honor, since she was a very strict and demanding disciplinarian. So taking Sylver to dance classes was a natural way to raise her, given my affinity for dance.

I love dancing! I used dance training to rehabilitate myself from a back injury during my first trials with disability in the late '70s when my doctor suggested I try dance classes to restore my physical functioning and also to loose weight.

I had gained 25 pounds eating cookies at work. It was not quite that simple. The point is that I was dually motivated. So I danced my way back to health. It worked.

When the time had come again to overcome physical disability, Dr. Adams reminded me of this resource. In no time, I found Synergy Dance that led me to polarity therapy.

As fate would have it, Linda Verrill had just passed away when these tragic circumstances were happening. It was at her funeral in a conversation with her daughter, another committed dancer, that I learned of SynergyDance. The window closed and the door opened.

I suspect that Linda was there in spirit to pass on the baton. She was one of my favorite people. She embraced me with a lot of love and compassion. She was a marvelous role model. She danced until the day she drew her last breath and lived to be in her 70s. Her home on Connecticut Avenue, NW, was sacred space for Sylver, Katherine and me. Linda would also be Sylver's first dance teacher in Washington when we moved to the area.

SynergyDance is the brilliance and genius of Charmaine Lee. Later in this book, I will share a few details. It is sufficient to say here that Charmaine understood the meaning of healing movement. If you are reading this book and need to try something new and expansive, consider this option. A whole new paradigm for dance therapy, this is where the energy medicine story begins, in a dance class.

I remember the first experience of energetic movement that I sensed clearly in my body. I was lying on my back on the floor in a SynergyDance class reviewing some movements with my future myotherapist, Michele Macomber. And it happened! I felt it and saw it! My left pelvis sank toward the floor beneath me in external rotation without any conscious effort of which I was aware. Eureka! I felt it! I *knew* something life changing was happening to me in that instant.

The place in my being that I discovered that day has become my new resting place. In the spaces in that place, I know that God conquers all and that miraculous healing is possible. It was my first experience of the Breath of Life before I knew about energy medicine principles.

I joyfully attended SynergyDance classes because I got results, even when it was painful and difficult. Cumulatively, I felt better than ever before and got stronger and more limber. My threshold for pain and actual pain perception were reduced by my participation in SynergyDance classes over time. At the height of my studies, I religiously attended classes three times a week. I also became a bodywork client of Charmaine, the creator of SynergyDance. She would be my first polarity therapist and the first to unveil the extent of my dissociative tendencies.

It was on Charmaine's treatment table that I first recall completely separating from what I could not face. She told me how badly fractured I was and how much I needed to stay in therapy until I found some relief and some answers. I am greatly indebted to her magic and to her understanding of her craft. I will always practice SynergyDance. It saved my life.

But, all good things, indeed, can have some very sad endings. My tenure in class would be no exception. The facility would close, and the new location would preclude my attendance on a regular basis. So I stopped taking classes, much to my dismay. I studied other movement disciplines, including continuum and tai chi. All the movement forms I practiced taught me great lessons. They are stable resources in my ongoing regimens.

Through all my trials, I learned a great deal about the seasons that come and go to teach us what is necessary for our complete journey. Some learnings and lessons come for a single season, some come for all seasons. Knowing the difference is a key distinction and an essential part of discernment in the healing process.

The name changes: Fibromyalgia is born!

Now we have myofascial trigger-point disorder, cold sensitivity, depression, panic disorder, dysthymia, agoraphobia, "doctor-phobia," pharmaceutical toxicity with insomnia, constipation, irritable bowel syndrome (almost forgot the return of this one) and dissociative tendencies. Nothing has been said about fibromyalgia.

Thought I had forgotten? Truth is, in the beginning, there was no fibromyalgia. Or at least medical science didn't call it that.

The name myofascial trigger-point syndrome somehow just didn't get the starring role in this drama. When the time came to classify my pain disorder with Worker's Compensation after my case was argued and tried and accepted two years after it was filed, the name was officially registered as fibromyalgia. It was the accepted label for the medical community at the time for the medical condition associated with my complaints. It was 1992, four years after onset.

My initial reaction to this name change was to be angry. I thought the original name was more accurate. My rather moralistic, perfectionist personality had a hard time reconciling a less than perfect diagnosis and nomenclature.

"Why was this necessary?" I argued.

I still did not seem to understand the ways of the world and the requirements for getting along without rocking the boat. But my offense at the name change would be the small stuff in the scheme of the bureaucratic maze that I would travel through as my injuries mounted.

To avoid confusion, myofascial trigger-point disorder would disappear from the language in my medical reports. It would reappear years later when I learned that some experts believe there are actually two similar conditions or related syndromes, but they are not necessarily the same thing. I had believed this all along.

My belief about this probability of two different medical conditions triggered some of the anger I carried within. My pain was very specific at onset; there was no generalized flaring in my whole body. Only certain muscle groups were affected. And while I had much referred pain, I was not in pain all over 24/7, at least not at the beginning. The pain was localized for at least the first six to eight months, maybe longer. I know of many sufferers whose sole complaint consisted of generalized pain without trigger-points. But none of that matters, really. Fibromyalgia became the "accepted" melting pot for all. My case for disability was decided on that condition with the notation, "aggravated by cold sensitivity," to account for the on-the-job injury.

But none of this is the point. It is only the story of how I came to have this particular diagnosis. And while the Worker's Compensation evaluation process was one of the primary perpetuating factors of my dis-eases, I probably will only make references to it in this writing. I am not sure that I am ready to tell that entire story yet!

The future was born. I was identified with a group of very suspect sufferers of what has been called "pain that never goes away." Fibromyalgia was truly no saving grace upon its identification. Many chaffed and scoffed and boldly called me names, accusing me of making unfounded, impossible, illogical claims. Why was I wasting my excellent mind on the pursuit of such nonsense and folly?

"No one could be in pain all the time and look like her," they opined.

My quest for wellness was an uphill battle all the way. But then everybody had fibromyalgia by the late '90s. So I would become part of the new wave just as my pioneer archetype required. I had defended my dis-ease for over ten years. It was an "I told you so!" moment for justPaula.

In 2014, there is a commercial on television advertising a prescription drug for the treatment of fibromyalgia. When I first saw it, I was overcome. I wept gently.

My experience with muscle pain would give new meaning to the idea of manifesting a medical condition. I have no doubt that I was an early guinea pig for many who treated me, especially as it relates to injections. I don't think that most of the doctors who gave these treatments believed that they worked, just as they did not believe that the condition existed. It is the only explanation that I can live with. It is better than thinking they were all too lazy to get it right or just did not care if the injections worked. Of the five or six doctors who injected me, only one knew how and followed through with all phases of the protocol. Only one prescribed the specific passive stretches for each muscle or muscle group and used the stretch and spray procedure post injection. Dr. Reynolds was the only one!

So now the lineup is complete, fibromyalgia/myofascial trigger-point syndrome complex, cold sensitivity, panic disorder, depression, dysthymia, dissociative tendencies, agoraphobia, "doctor-phobia" with associated insomnia, constipation, irritable bowel syndrome and toxicity. It is just too much to say in one sentence. It is too much to think about, not to mention too much to treat.

Mostly, these dis-eases and diagnoses represent a vicious cycle of imbalances in the core of my being. Imploded anger tops the list and traumas too numerous to absorb held that anger deep in my body-mind. Fractures in all the places that make a human being whole created dis-eases in all the spaces that organize my life force. How far did I stray away from the midline of my being? How pervasive was the autonomic overload? Can my nervous systems be normalized? Will I ever be pain free? Of course, all these dis-eases led to many questions. Fortunately for me, I found ways to explore these questions that would teach me Truths way beyond my wildest imaginings. Again, energy medicine led the way.

The minor challenges—digestive imbalances, insomnia, and severe toxicity—were the first to go in my long-term treatment plan. Once I started detoxing meds in 1996 and changing my diet and finding the magic of supplements, I began to shed layers of discomfort one-by-one.

I invested in an organic diet and consulted a clairvoyant nutritionist, Kimberly Miles, who is another important link to my recovery and wellness. I was saddened when she left the D.C. area and look forward to her return. She is now writing in Sedona.

From a base of detoxing meds and embracing energy medicine, I engaged things that worked for me and that manifested my healing grace. If you will recall the emergency room visits I described earlier, I literally went from the hospital to the classroom on one of those fateful panic days. My date with destiny began with me propped up on pillows sitting on the floor in a polarity therapy training. From that place on the floor, I would rise to great healing heights.

Before I close this chapter, let me say, for the record, that this is not a medical report intended to teach medical facts. This is a spiritual story about an individual journey through a series of medical mysteries and manifestations. The story is intended to enlighten and inspire others to seek the truth about their very special healing challenges. What I learned from the evolution of these diseases and diagnoses was to persevere and seek my answers from within the best support and external resources that I could find. I prayed a lot and made a lot of mistakes along the way. It was a difficult and life-threatening journey. But as God became clearer, my way became brighter. I found all the ways I could help myself! I also found my *knowing* self, and that has made all the difference.

CHAPTER 4

The Great Taboo

FROM THE JUSTPAULA POEM: *ATTACK!*

Panic! Panic!
In my brain!
Come and Go!
And come again!

Water! Water!
Need to drink!
Help me!
Cause I am on the brink!

Almost here,
Almost there
And somewhere in between.
Of the darker realms of life
Somehow I am the queen.

Why I ended up on a life path with "crazy" as a primary theme is a question that baffles the mind in many ways, regardless of how I got here. There are probably as many versions or interpretations of why I am who I am as there are participants in the events themselves. For sure, if you asked my mother or sister or daughter to tell these stories, another series of writings would emerge. However, I feel that my version has value-added for the soul's journey only I could experience in this lifetime. What I know for sure is that I have to write my stories down so that I can see what I am trying to say. After more than a decade of therapy, I now see that my personal experiences with the stigma of crazy are more palatable from the pen than from the couch.

What I like about my life in 2014 is that it is no longer totally structured around the next bodywork session or set of treatment effects. I am not always proud of the fact that I spent years in layers of confused states of grace, clamoring for any glimpse of clarity. Yet, I can boast victory over much brokenness and pain that no longer threaten my quality of life and living. Crazy has been an amazing teacher and a powerful healer.

I get to be integrated and conscious, creative and prosperous for a significant part of this amazing incarnation that I call myself and, yes, sometimes my selves. No matter what facets of my personality take the lead, the fractured pieces of my Spirit clench into place often enough for daylight to prevail and even pervade my life. This is the essence of my story! Black became light and gray became okay or just the next mountain to climb. In 2014, I am retooled, resurrected and ready to receive all the joys life has in store for me. Adversity is inevitable, but as I said in an earlier chapter—*God Is Bigger.*

I now realize that every day the good and the bad are all for the good no matter how things appear in the moment. My spiritual core determined and strong gave God a chance to change the script for my life. The crazy season was a necessary nuisance essential for me to embody grace from an illuminated space. I learned to see inside myself with my own two hands and an inquiring intention after years of study and practice in energy medicine. With deep states of stillness and wide perception as a reference point, I experienced miraculous healings that often defy explanation. I felt my Health (capital "H") in ways that not only reduced my pain and disability but also made me grow spiritually younger at the same time. My self-healing potential grew in quantum leaps through all my trials and tests of discipline and perseverance.

My doctor of 25 years stared at me in utter amazement as the progress of my healing process unfolded. He told me many times, "Just keep doing what you are doing!"

I could always feel his heart smiling through the puzzled look on his face.

Year by year, I detoxed from meds, stretched muscles and realigned structure with one phenomenal success story after another. I also had setbacks, usually emotional or psychospiritual. Only occasionally was the cause of a relapse due to physical re-injury in the last five years of my robust healing process.

I always found some way to bless myself with a healing experience. I always believed recovery was possible. Maybe sometimes the state of crazy enables one to see beyond the horizon. I did!

But before I saw the light, I created a monster. I guess I could not have picked an uglier MO for my mental dis-ease than panic disorder—at least in my way of thinking. What a shameless experience as a human being it is to be so fearful and afraid that you think you are going to die. The voice in my head shouted this menacing thought over and over again when I was in the pitch of a panic attack. What could create such a place in the psyche? Why do we need this phenomenon called panic to apologize for our autonomic, "fight or flight" behavior?

The Great Taboo—*Crazy!*

So this book is about a taboo subject: "crazy." No one talked about it back in the day and no one talks about it enough to make a real difference in 2014. I am not talking about it either, or so I thought, at least not as my ordinary everyday self. I believe my higher self is using her voice now that the veil of shame is lifted.

Many people adopt a hush-hush attitude when it comes to dealing with people like me who carry the label of crazy. They think somehow they are protecting the innocent. Sufferers whose journey it is to wade through the challenging territory of insanity and mental instability are most often innocent victims of life's injuries, karmas and contracts. Yes, even our sacred contracts often require us to endure the worst of times.

In the stories that I tell, crazy is used as a generic term for what most people understand, in the vernacular, to be unstable, abnormal mental or emotional behavior, if you will allow me a few liberties. I want to be clear here that I am not speaking as a psychiatrist or other physician trained in mental health diagnosis and treatment. I have been on the couch perhaps more than the average person. I have experienced crazy more often than I care to remember. Wading through the murky waters of depression, dysthymia, panic disorder and dissociation has obscured the light since I was very young. However, now I get to help others who have not benefitted from my successes with the treatment of these medical conditions that carry such a damning label as *crazy*.

Crazy is an idea with individuated as well as collective understandings. In some ways, this well nuanced word is the most unclear, overused word that I know. Most of us have been called crazy at some point in our lives. "Are you crazy?" is a frequently asked question in our culture. It might apply to an action that is just a bad idea or it might describe a heinous, unforgivable intent or injury. Sadly, the word, crazy, may also be used to stigmatize the human condition. Regardless of its use, this very familiar term means complex things that matter to the human spirit. That is why the word "crazy" is the impetus to the writing of this book about *Yesterday When I Was Crazy*.

One of the greatest obstacles to recovery for individuals whose lives are clouded by the ravages of severe emotional or mental illness is finding help or support from professionals who believe they can have curative impact. Very few therapists are skilled at reading the needs of "mental" clients or providing more than a Band-Aid for the medical symptoms, i.e., insomnia, anxiety and depression. There is too much reliance on drugs and chemical balance with little regard for experience or life balance.

I cannot imagine an illness without an emotion. In my opinion, there is an integral emotional and mental challenge for every physical challenge and most often a related spiritual imbalance as well. One should always ask or be asked how he or she thinks and feels about any injury or abuse and what it means in his or her life. There is always a connection. There is always a reason or cause for the difficult stuff that happens in our lives whether it makes perfect sense or not. Sometimes it is the soul-self yearning to be healed that is seeking our attention.

So why pretend that it is just an arm or just a toe or just a little scratch? Why not ask, "Why am I hurting myself and having lots of little accidents?"

Sometimes the "message in the madness" is simply to slow our pace a little or to have more fun or get some rest or breathe more deeply. Sometimes little nicks in the fabric of our lives are truly the small stuff. Other times, the cumulative impact of seemingly small events is leading to complete devastation.

Consciousness probing inquiries can go a long way toward reconciling the differences between major and minor events in our lives. More important, soul-searching activities can often lead to identifying and applying the most appropriate remedy or resolution. Forward progress may be dependent on opening doors to greater awareness and even greater mysteries that seem to elude us.

Get over it!

"Just get over it!" they say.

I say, "What exactly is it and how do I get over it—climb, crawl, walk, run, scream?"

By and large, I had very little skill at getting over it. Of course, I am referring to the things that made me crazy. I was far too adept at getting angry. Others I have noticed are experts at getting even or getting all for themselves regardless of who gets hurt.

The conditioned way of coping with an injury is to hide it and to shove it under the bed and pretend it didn't happen. This is especially true if the abuse makes one look weak or less than society's expectations. Heaven forbid that I should be viewed as disloyal to an employer or family member or spouse—even when I have been wronged by one of them.

The consolation postures of silence, secrecy and shame hang on like karmic debts. Our prayer is that the pain will disappear in time without any effort on our part. It is not generally understood that trauma can be held in the body and mind for a lifetime and even many lifetimes. Most individuals do not believe that seemingly "normal" life events—like family fights—can literally make us sick! There is a tendency to rationalize . . . "He didn't hit me hard!"

Personally, I never liked physical violence of any kind and was taught as a child not to fight. My siblings and I were forbidden to fight for any reason. The idea of "two for one"—spankings, that is— was frightening to my already abused psyche. The parental rule was that if you got a spanking at school you could expect another one when you got home—for getting the spanking at school.

No one taught me how to negotiate with my avengers or how to cope with bullies.

"Whatever you do, don't fight," was the only accepted code for the president's daughter.

"Thou shalt not fight back" was all I knew. Passive resistance was the only recourse for youngsters like me whose peers might just be waiting for an opening to engage in a royal smack down. Thank goodness there was no cell phone or YouTube in my day!

So every day the little boy hit me when I passed him in the hall at school, just like clockwork. Love taps they called it back then. I just kept on walking.

Why didn't I report these attacks? It did not help! Nobody cared about the woes of the privileged. Teachers and even my parents reasoned, "She is spoiled, she must have done something to him."

School authorities did nothing about bullies in those days. My parents did nothing. I soon learned to be a coward and to be nervous all the time. I started having fainting spells in the lunch line and developed sweaty palms and a "nervous stomach." Already, I did not like to eat good food and stole sugar from the sugar bowl on a regular basis washed down with Coca-Colas. Sugar was my friend—or so I thought.

Then one day, a couple of playground angels who had watched and witnessed my daily portion of violence had enough. Thank God! On this day, as I was rounding the corner of the school building on my walk home, I noticed my two heroes holding the enemy on both sides. As the enemy squirmed, the heroes encouraged me to "Come and get him!" and urged me, "Go ahead, hit him!"

I was confused and stunned at first. "How did this happen?" I asked no one in particular.

Yet, right before me was a once in a lifetime opportunity for payback. So hit him I did. In a hurried frenzy, I struck a few good blows to the chest of my torturer and ran home as fast as my strong dancer legs could carry me. My school was only a few blocks away, so home was not very far to run. Needless to say, the little boy never hit me again. The ones who helped me not only saved the day but also delivered me from a daily hell. For once, I was defended by someone who cared.

My elementary years were fraught with similar harrowing experiences of bullies and deliverances. I imagine that I was angry and afraid most of the time for one reason or another. I did not understand the hatred and violence. After all, I was born smart thanks to my genetically gifted parents, so I was told. It wasn't my fault! I didn't do anything wrong! By the time I reached high school, I had learned to handle personal attacks by shutting down, becoming mute and not responding at all.

Unfortunately for me and others like me, the necessity for and art of getting over it in a healthful manner was not taught in schools or most homes in those days—as far as I have observed. So there is no clear guidance on what it means in reality.

Letting go of hurts that hold one hostage is an intangible idea at best. Far too often, the response to injury is the knee-jerk reaction to seek revenge and to rebuke the idea of forgiveness or reconciliation. There are too few role models teaching us about self-healing or cleansing designed to free us from toxic energies that get stored in our bodyminds.

The messages from the environment around us are of no help either. "You fell down the stairs, again?" the mother inquires.

Or the teacher asks, "You still on crutches, girl?"

Or the abuser says, while slapping your face, "I do this because I love you! Just get over it! It is just a love tap!"

Or the boss observes, "It's just a broken leg, not cancer! It's not that serious!"

Or the lover demeans you and claims, "It's just words!"

Is the human spirit designed to defend against such disgraceful treatment? I would never underestimate the potential of the human spirit to overcome adversity. Is the human spirit intended to live this way? I don't think so!

So then, why is there so much acceptance of this type of hurtful conditioning in society? Why do solid citizens observe with a "blind eye" the injustices perpetrated against loved ones and neighbors every day? Why do "sheeple" (a new word I learned today) prefer the bandwagon to the truth, always going along with the crowd? Human rights are denied while gun rights are upheld in modern times.

Cruelty is accepted practice. Intolerance for the negative effects of mean-spirited acts of punishment or revenge is not growing fast enough. Abuse is prevalent all over the world. Young children are neglected and subjected to unrealistic expectations that at some level make us all "mental" and all "crazy."

Parenting has become the art of "Mini-Mes," the ego's dream. Adolescents are expected to follow the passions of their ancestry. Otherwise, offspring who try to break out of the parental mold are disowned and disenfranchised. Young adults are rejected when they make alternative or progressive lifestyle choices .

This is not to suggest that family traits and continuity are not worth carrying forward. Certainly, there is notable lineage that has uncanny propensities that prosper throughout generations. The education gene that dominates my family tree is an example of a beneficial legacy worth repeating. I am grateful!

What is important to consider in this narrative is that the list of imprints on the human spirit that can result in injury is not only endless but often viewed as part of a "normal" life. There are also endless choices each of us can make to shift the impact of our actions from ones that insult and create apathy to those that support and heal and create peace.

No person is considered above the potential for violence, including murder, under the right conditions. How could loving creatures have such lethal potential and survive? I submit that none of us will survive much longer with any quality of life if members of our society won't and don't outlaw cruelty and crimes against fellow humans and all creation for that matter. It is essential that all people everywhere express the lovingness that heals each other in our own heads, hearts, homes and communities.

Those who live with the stigma of emotional or mental illness know all too well, *it ain't just us!* We are not the only people walking around with disturbing thoughts and behaviors. Like "Janet from another planet" in one of my favorite soap operas, *All My Children,* I think the mentally suspect see the madness in the world even more clearly. I also know it is hard to live with the pain of it. So coping turns to avoidance and denial and anything else that rationally or irrationally helps keep the light from fading completely. Drugs, sex, music, food, work, play, all keep the music playing when the mind and heart can't find another connection. There is always the need for connection, connection to Source energy, whatever one believes that to be.

Craniosacral therapy, the biodynamic model, which I have studied and practiced for over a decade, postulates an energetic midline in the center of the physical body. It is a subtle expression of our energetic connection to Source—palpable by trained hands. This energetic midline integrates and organizes life experiences in the body. My work with this midline phenomenon in my own body has taught me a great deal about how we can feel the imbalances caused by a diminished connection to Source energy.

This frontier of opportunity to understand my inner self has strengthened my sense of connection to and awareness of Source or primary energy, I think, for all time. I can reclaim my midline any time I feel crazy or disconnected. At worst, I can know that I am away from it and apply resources to correct my state of being. I trust both the idea and the experience of the energetic midline. I trust it to tell me the truth and to lead me home.

I am blessed beyond words to have this perceptive ability notwithstanding the fact that it, too, falls into the category of The Great Taboo. Even in 2014, energy medicine modalities are not fully accepted practices. But one thing I know for sure is that one day they will be. So I will pioneer my way through the unfolding. And when, at last, I grace the old rocking chair, I will tell all, "I told you so!"

Who Said It?

Before I go any further, I have to share my pet peeve as it relates to the way some folks view The Great Taboo of panic. In a nutshell, whoever said that a panic attack is not life threatening lied. This is personal stuff so I beg your pardon for letting this go right now! Plain and simple, whoever said it just lied! Surely that individual never had a severe panic attack. The language itself is life threatening. Anything that undermines the very fiber of the human spirit is much more than life threatening. Panic attacks are destructive and can often cause irreparable damage.

I will illustrate this point from my own experience of frightening thoughts swirling around in my head, taxing my body and endangering my life during my years of intense vulnerability. This is how it happened for me.

The fear button gets pressed, internal dragons fire away and a vicious cycle of unbridled terror begins. Irrationality abounds and nothing feels safe. No one can be trusted, except maybe my dogs, if I am so fortunate as to have them nearby. Breathing is labored and has a jagged edge. My heartbeat is felt almost everywhere in my body. My mind races and rages against trigger memories and thoughts. Shadows are all around. All my muscles are tight. I feel safe only in the fetal position—or so I think. As long as no one around me moves or speaks, no one gets hurt. Shush! The voice of total confusion speaks independent of the spirit:

Don't touch me! I am afraid of everything!

Don't come too close; I might not understand your intention.

I might attack you! Stand back from me!

I am not rational.

I can't breathe! Help! No don't help!

I am confused. What is going on here?

Why am I doing this? Why am I afraid?

Wait! Listen! Did you hear that?

Okay. It's safe.

Well, maybe not.

I don't know. Think I'll sleep now.

No, No, not now.

They might come to get me!

I'm gonna die! I know I'm gonna die!

Water! Water! Water!

Give me a cigarette. I need a drink.

No, don't give it to me.

Yeah, give it to me.

It is better if I just pass out!

I'm gonna die!

I have vivid memories of driving down Georgia Avenue in Washington, D.C., while going into a full-blown panic episode, which lasted through several near accidents. Any of those potential crashes could have killed or maimed me. To this day, I do not recall the trigger or the ending or how I got home. Fortunately, my home was not far away.

Then there was the time I ran screaming out of the hospital after a session with a new therapist who kept telling me to "Just get over it." What I really needed to get over was her incompetence. She kept telling me that my medical history, which I chastised her for not reading, was not relevant to my treatment.

Just get over it! She continually admonished me verbally until the rage those words invoked sent me off into LaLaLand and off to the car to drive home. Another treacherous ride home followed that session. The smartest thing I had done in those days was to move close to the hospitals, the focal point of my life's work at that time. So home was not far. Or maybe angels were not far and grace was present, too. Or it just wasn't my time. Then I would not get a chance to tell this story and save other tortured souls from eternal damnation and humiliation—a life filled with life-threatening moments.

I now understand that whatever may have triggered my panic attacks, those moments were filled with uncertainty about my life and my well-being and safety. My God-given defense system went into overdrive as it had learned to do from so many such moments. A pattern of defensiveness was activated that was innate to my autonomic nervous system, called the fight or flight response.

A primitive response, no less, science tells us this internal mechanism was created in humankind to ensure our survival in the wilderness of life as cave dwellers. In that state, the blood rushes to the extremities and the body prepares to run away from danger. Breathing becomes shallow and the heart races to keep pace with the fight or flight—and the panic spirals out of control. There is also a "freeze" response to fear and danger. It is a state of sensory overload associated with playing dead or standing perfectly still like a deer in the headlights. The body becomes motionless as though physically paralyzed.

In my case, I would get ideas in my mind that I was about to die, literally, as I said earlier. In extreme attacks, depending on the activating event (as they say in biofeedback training), I might fight anyone who came near me or get confused about where I was and what was happening to me. I never thought, "Oh, I am just having a fight or flight response."

For most of my early years as a panic disorder sufferer I did not know about the fight or flight response. Interestingly, only one of my traditional therapists seemed to be trained to deal with it— although he did not emphasize this very much in our biofeedback sessions. I learned more about this innate response pretty much on my own by reading books and ultimately in my energy medicine classes much later in my healing process.

In most people's minds, I was just "going off." I was already thought to be an interesting bird, if you know what I mean. Erratic behaviors seemed to go with my already strange personality. I was the same lady that was claiming to be in pain 24/7—very suspect, indeed. I was just acting out because I was crazy anyway. Oh that's justPaula was an all too familiar tune.

So my life was threatened again and again. The fibromyalgia pain and disability always got worse after each panic attack. I lived in a constant state of hyperarousal. I became very cautious about the circumstances under which I would drive a car. The world became a debilitating burden. At the height of frequency of panic attacks, I truly never knew when a severe episode would come from nowhere and send me over the edge in what felt like a moment's notice. My willingness to take risks was impaired and thwarted and the beginnings of agoraphobia manifested.

Then yesterday would become today, tomorrow and the next day, until I wasn't crazy any more.

Panic attacks allowed me to be crazy just momentarily, for a few hours and often, depending on severity, for days. Added to complications related to fibromyalgia/myofascial trigger-point syndrome complex, the residual effects of a serious episode often lasted a couple of weeks. The contracted pressure on my already otherwise unhappy nerve and muscle tissues and trigger points always yielded the same results—physical terror. Compression of nerves equals pain, especially if you are already in pain.

Pain is quality-of-life threatening. Add panic and the territory expands. So the vicious cycle would spin its bitter weave of confusion. As I came back from the total unreality of pain aggravated by panic, I would swim through layers of emotional turmoil called depression and dysthymia, more safety nets that did not make sense. The threat of danger would linger in my spirit for days. Then the cycle would end. The pain would subside and I would return to myself almost as abruptly as I had gone away. The monster returned to the closet. All was calm. Yet, the witnesses were still as bewildered as I was about what happened and why, though I was grateful for peace if only for a while.

So I guess it depends on how you define life and what you consider threatening when pondering the seriousness of this great taboo often misread as crazy. Whatever one may believe, panic attacks destroy lives. Since all life is connected, they diminish the integrity of the Universe.

Many people like to suggest that the panic reaction is based on a "perceived" threat so it is not serious.

They say, "You only think you are going to die. There is nothing organically wrong. You'll be fine when it is over!"

Such doubting individuals have probably never lived through a panic attack or been truly sympathetic to anyone who has had one in their presence. For sure, these skeptics have never driven a car at the onset of an episode either.

Mental illness, yes, I said mental illness, is serious in any form. It sucks the light out of life in ways that mystify all our senses. Observers can become agitated and uncomfortable when confronted by the actual experience of a so-called "mental" event.

Somehow, panic attacks are viewed as suspicious behavior.

Considering the outward appearances, this analysis is understandable. Anytime breathing is impaired, anxiety and fear seem to kick in quickly. Unfortunately, panic attacks also seem to interfere with our inclinations to respond lovingly.

Most people I have met get weary of panic attack sufferers and would rather not be bothered with trying to help the crazy ones who just need to get over it. Now who is crazy? Or maybe apathetic souls are just inconsiderate by nature—nothing personal—or uninformed? Maybe they are looking in the mirror and seeing themselves—waiting to explode. Maybe someone in his or her life "played crazy" and made it bad for the rest of us.

So I am writing about this taboo subject to shed some light and to invite further inquiry and oodles more compassion for sufferers. Lots of folks just don't know very much about things they have no reason to know about. Others just want to believe the worst because it makes them look superior to the "special" people.

What I know for sure is that—Love is the answer! A kindly, supportive presence to the one who is suffering a panic attack can lead to peace in time.

Again, I speak from experience as I write about the lovingness that heals. I will share another miraculous story to make this point more picturesque.

The setting is yet another craniosacral therapy class in the year 2000. Our course work was nearing completion. The teacher was reviewing our testing procedures, which means I was already a little on edge. Test anxiety is lurking and waiting to rise up and spoil my day. This testing nemesis wreaked havoc on all my school years although it did not prevent my success as a student. Thank God!

Upon learning that our testing procedures had been altered and expanded, my "fright to flight" response got called to attention. Simultaneously, a fire alarm sounds in the classroom building. An intense vibrational charge surges up and down my central core like a

30,000-volt electrical charge to my nervous system. Panic arises. I flee from the classroom and find my way to a bench in a corner on the first floor. I remember running down the stairs to find safety somewhere close by.

Recognizing from past experience that I should not drive, I sat in secrecy waiting for calm to return. In shock from the velocity with which the panic attack occurred, I was in disbelief. I was nowhere near home this time. I was many miles away in another town in Maryland. I sat in silence hoping to be invisible until the worst was over, trying to remember to breathe consciously.

Thanks to the providence of mentors nearby, help was on the way. A gifted therapist who was a teaching assistant that day suddenly appeared in my view from my corner hideaway. Although my head was downcast, I could see and feel her loving presence only inches away. She sat down beside me in perfect stillness—not too close and not too far—just right.

Negotiating space with a client is the first rule of thumb in energy healing practice. She understood very well what was required. I recognized her proficiency in my subconscious observance of her behavior.

A highly skilled practitioner, the assistant knew the power of the Long Tide—an energetic layer of the Breath of Life—to restore order to primary human energy systems. Better yet, she knew how to access this healing resonance so that I would experience a reorganization of my life forces that had gone awry.

This amazing rescue by the teaching assistant was an energy medicine miracle in action. It was an example of one of the greatest lessons we learn in our studies in craniosacral therapy. In brief, Long Tide energy is known to express itself in tissues in the body as a transmutation of the Breath of Life. This sometimes shimmering, quality of energy is said to vibrate beyond trauma and to re-integrate the disturbances that trauma precipitates.

I know this is heavy stuff! Just ask any craniosacral therapist! We all marvel at the magical nature of this healing phenomenon.

In my mind, the Long Tide is God-energy and an expression of the "quality of lovingness" that the human spirit imbibes naturally. The Long Tide is the rhythm that keeps us connected to our Source, to quote Roger Gilchrist from his *Overview of Craniosacral Biodynamics,* an important resource in the process of healing overwhelming experiences. This self-healing dynamic for sure embodies the idea of amazing grace.

I am not certain how long this healing process with the teaching assistant lasted. It felt like forever at first. Although I probably was not tuned in to what she was doing in those early moments, she was someone I trusted.

As the irrational fear eased away, I came back to a more gentle countenance, grateful to my colleague and with even greater reverence for the Long Tide. A fellow practitioner, I knew about this powerful Intelligence (big "I") with which humans are endowed. Until this day, I had not had such a profound example of the Long Tide in action from the point of view of a panic attack. Awe and wonder lifted me up and restored me to some sense of normalcy. I was able to drive home safely without injury. I would ultimately pass my final exams with flying colors!

Sometimes I would like to say to God that He did not need to work so hard to teach me all these wonderful ideas about health and healing. But who am I to question God or my Soul or even my overwhelming challenges? Experience is the best teacher, they say. I say my goal as a storyteller is to let my experiences teach others so they do not suffer as much and as long as I did. It is my prayerful intention to relieve suffering in our world.

And now I know—It's academic!

My greatest experiment with The Great Taboo would occur a year or so later in my new home in D.C. on an auspicious day. It was another opportunity to view my panic experience through the perception of a craniosacral therapist waiting to change my life forever.

Who knew that I would be cast as an observer of the brain in panic mode at its academic best? Who knew enlightenment could be so forgiving and so healing? How could it be that I was chosen to witness my own brain churning and churning and telling me all about the didactics of the panic experience in energy medicine terms? Perhaps it was all for that single moment in time that I came to understand the genius of the human energy systems. All my pain and suffering seemed to hinge on this monumental awakening to life inside the cranium. Energy medicine rocks!

It truly was the good, the bad and the ugly that July morning in 2002. The good news was that my daughter and I were moving into our new house on Gallatin Street, a dream fulfilled. We were given another gift of the Almighty's amazing grace.

It was the culmination of an arduous, step-by-step journey to freedom from rental bondage. I was finally the owner of a mortgage, as my sister Camille so aptly put it. Hurray for Paula and Sylver!

On the one hand, I was elated about closing the deal, getting packed and ready to unload. But the worst was yet to come before the end of the day.

Actually, I thought the very worst was already over. The Flagler Flood, a pivotal chapter in our path to the new residence, is fully chronicled later in this book. Suffice it to say for now that my daughter and I were severely traumatized and almost electrocuted by the mega-storm that stole our previous home from us. We did not plan to move or to buy a house. The Universe or fate or destiny, whatever you may call it, scheduled this event literally in the midst of colliding thunderstorms and raging floodwaters. But back to the main story about the day we moved into our new house. The flood story holds many important life lessons yet to be shared.

Alas, halfway through the unpacking, the mover decides to demand full payment and much more than the original contract. It was a defining moment! I lost control of my emotions and proceeded to share my not so pleasant opinion with the moving company president over the cell phone. He, of course, was not on location. So his boys were given the order to vacate the move if I did not pay in full immediately. They followed his command and sat on the back of the truck with Spartan postures.

It was raining all over my stuff, yet I managed to maintain my composure through this betrayal and the emotional injury that followed. I guess I had acquired another bushel of grace points in that moment. Or maybe my angels and spirit guides were hovering close by once again. In any case, I had enough money to cover the overage. I paid and continued to collect my valuables. Everything was unloaded from the truck.

It had been a long, meticulous and painstaking process to get to this point in our lives. From undeserved liens on my credit and the floodwaters that brought rats and ruin, from devils over our heads calling us names and tormenting us every day in our place of refuge, from an abyss of loss and trauma, we had been saved by the bell. After months of searching feverishly for days on end, we had found a new home, just in the nick of time.

A wonderful new sanctuary was mine and ours together. And now, one special idiot was turning one of the best events of our lives into one of the worst nightmares ever. My spirit was crushed!

The inevitable panic attack ensued. I could no longer contain or redirect my internal chambers. I was soon in my new basement slipping into hell once more. My breath was choking me and my brain was spasming and shouting obscenities at my Spirit. I was offended, angry and sad, all at the same time. I was hiding my shame in my basement so my daughter would not be afraid for me. Someone that I thought I could trust threatened my safety. My soul was screaming for solace inside my brain.

Miraculously, I remembered to breathe consciously. The breath seemed to be leading me somewhere important. I noticed my in-breath and my out-breath; and then it happened. Suddenly, I was peering inside my own cranium like an astutely present craniosacral therapist.

If you will pardon my anatomical references for a bit, my observances of the disturbing signals in my head took on academic proportions that informed my experience of panic beyond anything I had identified before in my clinical trials. The falx and tentorium and central nervous system (CNS) and fluids and neurons were firing around and about with fury. The usual recognizable patterns of energy movements were now unrecognizable. The chaos in the rhythms of the tissues and fluids felt familiar in a way I never thought possible to palpate distinctly. The anatomy of a panic attack was happening in my brain and I was observing it. More important, I understood its fury in energy medicine language. It was academic!

In spite of my not so stellar understanding of the scope of anatomy, my toughest lessons in my energy medicine studies, I knew what was happening. Imagine that! Soon I was no longer afraid. I might be crazy, but I was always good at the academic stuff. The valedictorian was having her say and a better day to boot!

I began to ask the questions a craniosacral therapist would ask of any brain that shared this wondrous experience. What is the CNS doing? Is the ram's horn pulsing back and forth on the central axis? Why do the fluids seem to be all over the place and not neatly flowing through the ventricles and sub-arachnoid spaces? What is the midline doing? Whoa! Where is the Health? The questions my teacher would ask calmed me and supported my healing experience.

As the overwhelm subsided, I realized that I had just witnessed my own brain and fluids in panic mode unlike anything I could have imagined. My training as a craniosacral therapist paid off big time!

My experience of a panic attack would never be the same again. That is not to say it would never happen again. But then I knew: It had become academic once I recognized how to observe it from an informed perspective. The Ahas! were singing in my head and setting the stage for me to become panic-free.

My most recent experience of a panic attack occurred three years after the move in August 2005 when Hurricane Katrina broke my dam as well as many others. My writing channel came to the light soon after. My storyteller life was also breaking through the shadows of shame that stifled my voice for so long. As of 2014, it has been almost ten years that I have been free of this Great Taboo!

I am not mad about it anymore. As far as I am concerned, the student was ready and the teacher came. Now the story is told! Wow!

One woman's experience

This is a story about one woman's experience of a dis-ease. It is neither medically necessary nor sufficient in and of itself to cure others. It is intended to help sufferers and practitioners understand and treat a life-threatening dis-ease, panic disorder.

In post-9-11 America and the world, anxiety as an illness has reached epidemic proportions. Some of us who were already living with stress-related medical conditions before 9-11 found our symptoms exacerbated in the aftermath of that tragedy. Those who survived Katrina on rooftops pleading for dry land and deliverance add to the critical mass of extreme trauma and anxiety precipitated on August 29, 2005, and thereafter.

My predispositions to exhibit symptoms of this complex medical condition started in early childhood I believe although I was not diagnosed until I was in my mid forties. People who acted out, as it was often thought about in the '50s when I was growing up in the South, were just crazy and needed to get a grip. I certainly never heard anybody talking about panic attacks when I was a child or even as a teen. Histrionics, hysterical personality, etc. etc., or just plain crazy were the standard labels.

Families were allowed one or two crazy people as long as they did not discuss it. Panic disorder was the Great Taboo. It was swept under the carpet, not talked about openly, much like homosexuality. This is not to say that all the crazy people were having panic attacks, either. I believe many manifestations came out of the same triggers depending on the peculiar dynamics of a person's genetics, lifestyle, karma or sacred contract.

I am not too sure that my related challenges didn't start preconception and at every stage thereafter in my earliest development as revealed in the Born Angry chapter in this book. These things I will never know for sure. Empirical evidence is not available to substantiate my claims of attribution about soul encounters. However, the longer I explore my experiences of this disorder the more I learn.

Perhaps I will live to see more than I know today in someone else's recovery efforts. Either way, my soul is satisfied to have come this far and to embody such a profoundly enlightening series of teachings on the subject of panic attacks.

This writing may be just the beginning of the unfolding of even more of the mysteries of the elusive nature of panic attacks. Yet I am right now in 2014 compelled to recount what I feel is useful about my involvement with this illness and various forms of treatment. It is my goal to empower those who are willing and ready to look more closely at their experience of panic disorder and heal.

CHAPTER 5

The Fall: The Dark Before the Dawn

I T IS 1988 IN THE NATION'S CAPITAL and I am a seven-year bureaucrat, hatin' life in my good government job! I have breathed and worked in a place of pervasive chaos for close to a decade. I am perhaps angry all the time about one thing or another. Mostly, I am appalled, hurt and embarrassed by my experiences and those of my colleagues and all that I witness on a daily basis. Discrimination, dysfunction and degradation are the order of the day and *status quo* is the code. *Hear no evil, See no evil, Speak no evil* are the policy.

I am in the midst of all of this chaos emerging as the voice of the program I represent. I am considered one of the resident experts. I had opportunities to develop training programs and strategies for improving information management and dissemination at the State Department of Education in South Carolina. I was employed as a program specialist long before I joined the federal service.

There was no Internet. Word processors were still in vogue in 1988. A good typist was an essential employee. Telecommunications were primitive at best.

Notwithstanding the enormity of any big task, I was fearless and passionate about all I surveyed. I was the classic type A personality with a little flavor or maybe a lot of flavor and stunning complexities.

I was a terrific organizer, if I do say so myself, so I always got to chair the big jobs. No one else really wanted the responsibility for these demanding top shelf assignments so I took the helm willingly. (Many of my colleagues thought I was crazy for taking the plunge into troubled waters a.k.a bureaucracy.)

In my mind, spearheading the big projects was a strategy to get step increases and ensure a great performance rating. I believed hard work was good for my future. I was an energetic, young, single parent with a household to maintain and a daughter to support. I was raised in a powerful family. I expected only the best for myself.

Well, I am sorry to say that in those days, the late '80s, much like the "ol' days," light-skinned blacks, a.k.a., people of color or Negroes who "looked white" like me, were persecuted *just dry long so*—as my father used to say. No good reason was needed to inflict racist acts against blacks of any hue in 20th century America. The one-drop-rule dominated the culture of discrimination. Invisible blackness, meaning anyone with one drop of Negro blood or African ancestry was classified as black. Pretty much everybody knew everybody else's racial makeup. The only way to avoid discrimination if you happened to be light-skinned was to pass for white and move away. Very few of us were up to that challenge or even willing to engage in such a charade. Most of us just lived with and through the confusion we stirred up.

Many people felt there were undeserved advantages given to lighter-skinned blacks. And perhaps many with lighter hues took advantage when given an opening. I cannot speak for all of us who lived in this race within the race. I can only speak for myself.

What I can say for sure is that being considered a racial outcast was not fun. Nor did I understand the treatment I received because of my light skin when I was a young child. I did not understand why people were so mean to me and always calling me by my skin color in terms I will not repeat here.

I learned to grin and bear it without retort, avoiding fights and cussing matches at all costs. Vengeful responses to name calling and bullying were punishable by the parents of the college president's daughter.

Colorism, as we define it in 2014, has been grounds for mistreatment or exclusion for ages. This, of course, is not news. Unfortunately, colorism is alive and well even now in the 21st century.

I was deeply moved by Michelle Obama's Kansas graduation speech commemorating the 60th anniversary of the Supreme Court decision, *Brown v Board of Education,* that integrated schools. She encouraged the next generation to "Ask the hard questions and have honest conversations about the wounds of the past to move forward to a better future."

Graduating seniors were reminded to never be afraid to talk about race even if they have to "ruffle a few feathers." I commend our courageous First Lady for her eye-opening reality check.

In order to heal the curse of racial inequality, it is necessary to talk about it—another Great Taboo! So my stories about racial identity are intended to be part of the sharing that is needed to cleanse our souls.

I was not a welcomed sight for most of my tenure in the federal service. It did not help that I was not charmed or impressed with the label, "Super Black," which one of my supervisors tried diligently to explain to me. He was serious, too! I was outraged! I understood that this label was not meant to compliment me on my skill set but to commandeer my loyalty as one of the "better thans" in my race based on my lighter hue. All of the other "Super Blacks" he grouped me with looked like me. My failure to play along with the powers that be was ultimately to my detriment when I got sick.

Based on my looks alone—silky hair, size 8, snappy dresser—I was a walking target. I recognized fully that more degrees of separation would not serve me well among my peers. I did not want to be called a "Super Black." It felt like a disservice to my race. I already had too many name tags to wear. So I said, "No, thank you," and bore the consequences of not going along with their program.

I made all this bad casting worse by being an outstanding employee with files of kudos from constituents and internal big wigs who almost never saw me in the flesh. One of the national workshops that I chaired and developed received such rave reviews that I was showered with letters from college and university officials and commendations from assistant secretaries in my department. I was proud and grateful for the recognition. I was always exhausted when the applause was over.

I possessed great perseverance, carrying out most of my feats of exceptionality in the background. The limelight was primarily for those with signature authority. Yet all this behind-the-scenes excellence came at a high price. I took work home far too often and fought saboteurs at every turn. High achievers did not garner much support or appreciation. Once again, I blew the curve. How dare I work so hard!

Eventually, the wear and tear from abiding so intensely in a valueless environment caught up with me. My soul started to crash and my body followed. I became numb to the constant challenges of an unfulfilling life. 21 years of single motherhood, abusive relationships and early life traumas set against the backdrop of invisible power and increasing work overloads took their toll. I start to exhibit sensations and symptoms that led to total brokenness and devastating losses.

Dis-eases and diagnoses, pain, panic and disability became the focus of my life as I outlined in Chapter 3. Hopefully, I provided you, dear reader, with just enough detail to set the stage for the unfolding of the miraculous healing process. It is my goal to highlight the victories of what worked. I pray the no-pain/no-gain strains in my narratives will pale in comparison to the stories about the lovingness that heals.

The "fall from grace" was humiliating, hard to fathom and seemingly never-ending. Ultimately, the same devastating path to brokenness led to resurrection to a higher order quality of life, liberty and awe, callings only Divinity could have ordered. So all would be well in my future. I just did not know it yet.

However, none of the dawning of an enlightened future unfolded before years of unsuccessful medical trials, setbacks, disappointments, despairing and exacerbating conditions ravaged my body, mind and spirit. The stories of tribulations alone could fill a book.

Day-by-day, week-by-week, month-by-month, year in, year out from 1988 until 2003, for 15 years, I tirelessly sought medical treatment. Even for the years I worked part-time after my illness started, my health or lack of it was my full-time occupation, a necessary priority just to get through the day.

My professional ratings dropped though my quality of work did not as the establishment looked with disgust over my fall from healthful productivity to wrestling with LWOP (leave without pay). I was conveniently inconvenient. As time marched on, I was no longer whole for 8 hours a day. My medical conditions worsened. Largely due to insults against my character and integrity, I could not battle my health challenges and the government, too. I was accused of using my brains to outsmart my employer so that I did not have to work. I was denied reasonable accommodations like a heater or an office without an air conditioning vent blowing over my head. I was ridiculed by supervisors who thought they were on to my "scheme."

All the while I cried out for help, just as befuddled as everyone else. The difference was that I was the one living with the pain, the disbelief and rejection. All of a sudden, the same skilled brain that brought showers of kudos became the enemy personified. I will never understand why it was necessary to demean a worker who had given so much to the work. But I am being naïve. Back to reality. Sorry!

I went to extreme lengths to keep working with dignity and quality, including taking work home and to the hospital when I had to go. (The later incidents drove my daughter batty—and rightfully so.) This is where I truly *was* the crazy one!

Few of my colleagues supported me or cared about my struggle with medical science or reality. Few people believed that I was sick. Most of my peers and associates thought I was just going crazy from all of the job stress, work overloads and bureaucratic treachery. It does happen. In their defense, their assessment was not so far-fetched—just unkind and, therefore, unloving.

By the time all was said and done, I did become emotionally, mentally and spiritually challenged in addition to physically disabled. The constant shocks to my core were more than I could bear. All that I strived for and believed in crumbled before my very eyes or, at least, I thought so then.

Eventually, through Congressional intervention, I prevailed and exited the federal service on full disability. I was bedridden and unable to perform any of my duties. This is the part of the story that I want to forget. However, all the struggles would be full of life lessons and miracles that would be part of my redeeming grace. I am grateful for all that I faced and all that I overcame.

It was 1992, the fourth year of my failing grace, that I was liberated from the tyranny of my employment. It was a blessing and a curse. I was free to seek my own healing solutions without obstacles precipitated by the battlefield experience at work. I was suffering and mostly alone, except for my beloved daughter, Sylver. I was reduced to a disability income. There would be no more step increases.

I am not done with my exit story. Just so you understand that mine was not an ordinary departure, there was one last ditch effort to keep me gainfully employed.

Just before the final curtain was drawn on my professional life, I was allowed to work at home under a special arrangement that had just been approved as a "reasonable accommodation." Eureka! I thought for sure the worst was over.

I was only 44 years old. I could not imagine losing my career and my future just because I was sick. I was once again totally naïve. Greater abuses of authority would follow before my traumatic work life ended abruptly.

Suffice it to say that the eleven months of the work-at-home arrangement almost elevated beyond repair my already impaired ability to communicate when threatened by individuals with major influence over my life. As of this date in 2014, there are no authority figures in that position anymore. I never tried that kind of structure again.

My employment ended with one of the many panic attacks triggered by events related to employee/employer interactions. I did not understand the nature of power letting and getting. Now I had given my power away or had it taken away. I was powerless in the face of panic, pain and passages I was experiencing that seemed to have no clear rhyme or reason. Nothing made sense any more.

I felt like all hope was gone. I was an abject failure. I was in the middle of a major life crisis. All of me was broken into smithereens. No job. No peace. No joy. No answers. No love.

It would take quite a few years of healing trials and miracles for me to recognize that all of the troubles I endured were leading me to new beginnings. The following years of focusing on dis-eases and diagnoses and doctors and clinics would yield a new way of being in my body, mind, and spirit and in the world. This pioneer was not through pioneering. She was starting anew. I forged ahead on a soul's journey with a sacred contract with healing that would revitalize my life and health for all time. SynergyDance and energy medicine led the way.

So before I conclude this chapter and tell my stories about my good doctors, I would like to add a little positive result from this sad story.

The work-at-home arrangement provided me with my first computer and my first experience with telecommunications. It was another challenge for justPaula. I put the whole thing together—hard drive, printer, installed software, etc.—by myself. This was a major feat for me. I am usually "all thumbs" with mechanicals, schematics and assembling electronics. Maybe I had a little help even then that I did not know about. Thanks, angels. Now I know it was you!

CHAPTER 6

The Good Doctors

I AM AWARE THAT I HAVE ALREADY HERALDED the names of my two favorite doctors—Drs. Adams and Reynolds. But this book would not be complete without a chapter devoted a little more specifically to their good works on my behalf. There is more to their stories.

I began to appreciate just how unimportant race is in the overall scheme of things the day I met Dr. Michael Reynolds, a rheumatologist extraordinaire. Since I am a product of the '60s, I took freedom of choice to the max when it came to doctors. I believed as I had been taught that black doctors understood Negroes (oops, I mean blacks) better than any others. So I always tried hard (admittedly) to find black doctors for all the serious stuff.

The opportunity to have a black doctor did not even exist in the town of Denmark where I grew up. There was one white doctor for everyone. Living in D.C., I took pride in the availability of qualified African-Americans in every branch of medicine. Then I was referred to Dr. Reynolds to solve the mystery of the chronic pain. His treatment of me would restore my faith in the races of man.

Dr. Reynolds, a very gifted Caucasian doctor, was practicing at, of all places, a black college hospital, Howard University, in Washington, D.C. He was a colleague of my primary care physician,

Dr. R. George Adams, who was my reference beam for my entire healing journey—a true Earth Angel.

The painful treatment that I would receive from Dr. Reynolds for six years would prepare me simultaneously for the worst of times and the best of times. I don't think I will ever fully comprehend how I came to embrace the painful trigger-point injections.

One of my strongest childhood memories is of running away from my family physician, Dr. Thomas, whenever it was my turn to get a shot. The nurses would have to chase me around the examining table and help hold me down while I received my shot, kicking and screaming. It was most embarrassing for my mother and siblings. But I was terrified of needles for reasons only a shaman or past life regression expert can understand. I now say that, even as a child, I knew what was coming down the pike.

Ironically, at my most painful, shots became my best friend. The only physician who knew how to administer them effectively became my other best friend. Of course, now the shots and the docs are my best friends of the past.

Dr. Adams was the first to honor my abnormal medical experiences and to believe they were real and not imagined. He was the first to show me the compassion of a true healer. He also encouraged me again and again to keep a journal and to tell my story. He was recently promoted to chief medical officer at Howard University Hospital, a well-deserved achievement.

This is not to say that all of Dr. Adams' referrals were successful. To the contrary, there were many unsuccessful attempts to find the right specialists. I can retrospectively thank one of them who taught me the greatest lesson of all: not to always believe what doctors say.

As I stated earlier, Dr. Doubt It, we will call him, another rheumatologist, told me that I would probably never dance again. He obviously did not know the dancer in me. But that is okay. I never let anyone tell me what I could or could not overcome after that. Dr.

Doubt It also taught me the value of a small handbag and to remember that my shoulders were not "beasts of burden." I preach this to my clients who haven't learned how to gracefully pull a wheelie bag.

Dr. Adams sent me to Dr. Reynolds in September of 1988. I finally got the diagnosis that would change my life forever.

Dr. Reynolds managed my case and my care with the skill of a scientist. His techniques were perfection. His documentation was of the highest order. Every muscle and every muscle twitch were recorded daily. Every passive stretch or isometric exercise was precisely calculated and executed. From my neck to my calves, Michael Reynolds poured milliliters of procaine through 2-inch needles that probed through my tissues while I looked the other way. It became routine after the first couple of years. And there were times the treatments were suspended because it was too much for me to endure, again and again, week in and week out.

Then there were the times I traveled miles away to Johnston, Pennsylvania, after Dr. Reynolds moved his practice there. It was worth the ride there and back to get the relief only his talented hands could provide. I would hire a driver for a day and ride up for my injections from the only physician who had the skill to help me. I rode home right after the treatment was administered. This gave me just enough time before the anesthesia wore off and the adverse effects kicked in that preceded the relief.

The insults posed by the needles easing through my tissues on the brink of all my nerves were almost unbearable. The healing crisis that ensued often left me crawling on the floor and crying out in pain. But in a day or so, my pain would be reduced just enough for me to feel human again, if only for a short while.

The temporary relief was worth it since nothing else worked. None of the medications could reduce the severe pain in 80 percent of my muscle and connective tissue. The trigger-point injections (as administered by Dr. Reynolds only) could give me relief for days as well as restore some of my daily functioning. The muscle retraining prescribed in the stretches and isometric protocols that supported the injections kept my tissues flexible and toned.

I was a very good student for most of my school days. It turned into one of my greatest assets during these early years of attempts at rehabilitation. So I learned to stretch body parts that I could not pronounce very well or even remember the names of most of the time. Dr. Reynolds was a good teacher. I learned to execute the exercises with great precision. I did not realize then, but these early trainings would set the tone for the years of rehabilitative trials that I would endure before I could reclaim my physical functioning. From trapezius to quadratus, sternocleidomastoid to minimus, I learned to stretch them all, one by one, and practiced each until I found the healing place. For sure, my life as a dancer inclined my musculature to cooperate so passionately.

Dr. Reynolds championed my cause. As synchronicity would have it, he was also editing the next series of books on the treatment of trigger-points with David Simons, M.D. I was a convenient guinea pig for Dr. Reynolds who was just writing the descriptions of exercises and treatment protocols as I was coming into the depths of my disease. I enjoyed that part of my relationship with him. It engaged my intellect and made me feel valuable and worthwhile. My suffering could at least benefit others.

For those who do not know anything about trigger-point injections, you can thank President Kennedy and his personal physician, Dr. Janet Travel. This treatment system she devised to treat Kennedy's back pain was, at first, a well-kept secret.

I would abandon these painful injection treatments myself in the future, primarily because I could not find another doctor who could administer them as well as Dr. Reynolds. Most attempts by other physicians actually caused me more pain and, in some cases, further injury. However, for six years, trigger point injections were the only real relief I experienced. This fact is still a little dizzying to recall. The blessings of all that I learned about muscular rehabilitation from engaging this treatment with Dr. Reynolds will be primary in my self-care regimen for all time.

Much like the injections, the side effects of the pharmaceuticals that I took for my dis-eases made most of them ineffective as long-term remedies. My daily life was constantly challenged by everything from blurred vision to digestive imbalances to mental confusion. I remember asking, "What good are these Rx's, if I can't see?"

Thankfully, as I look back on it now, I could not abide side effects and more or less had a zero tolerance for those that lasted longer than a few days. I already had a layer of mental confusion called, "fibrofog," which is associated with fibromyalgia. Adding another layer of fog due to pharmaceutical side effects really made me medically crazy! What became overmedication actually made me more and more symptomatic, toxic and miserable.

Ironically, this travesty against my health would also lead me to self-healing when I finally figured out that I was poisoning myself with prescription medicines. My Green Applesauce Saga later in this book will explain more fully my "detox or die" epiphany.

Sadly, there were very few people around me, professional or otherwise, who understood me or believed me when I talked about all that I was going through because of the mysterious pain that would not go away and could not be contained. I shudder to think how I would have survived had I not found Drs. Adams and Reynolds, not only to champion my cause, but also to save my life and stay the course for the 15 years that I underwent constant therapy. I never found any other physicians to replace or measure up to their support or belief in my case. That is a pretty scary thought even today as I write this.

I started treatment with several other private physicians, mostly physiatrists (pain and rehab experts). As described earlier, I even spent six months in a full time pain clinic. I made progress from time to time. Once I actually made great progress. Each time, I had major setbacks, usually involving the same practitioners that were treating me. Some betrayal would undermine any success I had made, and I would be back to square one.

Dr. Walter Bland, a psychiatrist at Howard University Mental Health Clinic, is an addition I would make to my good doctor list. Dr. Adams also recommended Dr. Bland. He would be a valuable asset to my recovery in the last years of my full-time treatment. Dr. Bland had oversight of the anti-anxiety medication that I was taking and gave counsel and support to my detox program and applications of energy medicine to my mental and emotional challenges. He was open and receptive and kind. I was blessed by his guidance.

Most of my good doctors were actually not doctors at all but practitioners of the healing arts in the latter years of my rehabilitation. The students in my energy medicine classes, the polarity and craniosacral therapists I sought privately, the SynergyDance, tai chi and Continuum teachers. Roger, Tom and Johnny, Charmaine, Michele the Miraculous and, more recently, High Priestess Thu-Hien Poma were and are all good doctors in my book. The *Oprah Show*, Caroline Myss, Deepak Chopra, Gary Zukav, Iyanla Vanzant, Andrew Weil and all the rest of the new age sages whose books I studied were good doctors, too.

A very special good doctor who holds a brightly smiling place in my heart and my healing process is my sister, Dr. Alma T. Young. She departed this earthly plane in 2012 as a legend in her field of social work. She was the first talk therapist to "hear" me and "listen to me" with lovingness. The referral to one of her colleagues, Marionette Daniels, would prove to be life sustaining. I know Alma is helping to carry me through this storytelling adventure with her halo shining brightly. Thanks, Sis!

So I guess the truth is that I had many "good doctors" to guide and direct my journey to healing. For this, I am deeply grateful.

CHAPTER 7

The Doggies:
Foster, Aria and Blanche

Foster, the first

WHEN I GOT FOSTER LOGAN POTTS, I was bedridden from a recent setback and had moved out of my home into the warm and cozy top floor of my cousin Rose's house. The heat in my house had been off, for much longer than my landlady suggested, three days I think. My pain was flaring fast.

It is significant that I actually had somewhere safe and warm to go. It was also quite remarkable that I actually went to that haven. By 1994, I was really used to being pretty confined. I was never really warm, so the lack of heat in the dead of winter was particularly painful.

I don't remember right now if I had electric blankets or space heaters. Those little heaters were not so available in the early '90s. Electric blankets were expensive and electrical power was in short supply in most places. Most people were not willing to take a chance that their electricity might go out. I did manage to finagle a Craftmatic bed with a heated pad at some point early in my medical trials.

All this notwithstanding, I had to leave home to have any hope of staying out of the hospital with one of those crazy panic attack spells.

About the same time my heat went AWOL, my daughter, in her efforts to comfort me proposed a healing companion, no less, for me to love. A four-legged friend. What a delightful idea! I was a captive audience.

Puppies and small dogs were among my favorite things for all my life. Pets were a joyous childhood memory even though we lost them sometimes yearly to car accidents on the main drag in front of my house on US Highway 1. Through all the back porch litters and back-yard funerals, doggies were my friends loyal and true. They made me laugh and smile more times than most humans. Their very presence had always rocked my world as if God, in the flesh, was present.

So Sylver brought what I affectionately call my "pieces of God," one-by-one. Foster Logan Potts, Ph.D., was the first. Small and silver on a black velvet blanket, a tiny miniature Schnauzer, Foster was delivered to me at cousin Rose's house in her warm and cozy living room.

There was one small problem though. Foster needed a place to pee and poop. Cousin Rose's spot was not for hire for that purpose. Wee-wee pads were an unknown commodity in those days. In any case, pads would probably not have mattered much to fastidious Cousin Rose, who was not a doggie girl. Baby, her beloved turtle, in a pen of water, very contained, was her cat's meow. No running around on the Orientals for my Foster Logan Potts.

So, of course, I had to go back home immediately. As destiny would have it, my heat was fixed the day following this blessed event. Foster Logan Potts could have his yard for frolic and functions of great importance.

My dad had trained us in the art of puppy management in my early childhood years in rural South Carolina, so I was not only grateful for my daughter's generous and insightful gift, I knew what had to be done to take care of business. Sylver and I had owned dog-gies on and off throughout our life together, depending on the rules of our dwellings. Little did I realize the healing gem that had been given to me. It would not be long before I would be keenly aware and dependent on my new best friend, Foster.

Day in and day out, I fed him and trained him. Sylver did the walking. Each day, he became smarter and smarter and invented a few moves of his own. I will never forget the moment he twirled into a circle of turns that became "turn around," our newest command. He could turn around once, two times and three times when he was feeling it. Foster could carry two balls in his mouth at once and "sit" and "shake," all of which I taught him with Sylver's help and support. Day in and day out, Foster Logan Potts never ceased to amaze us.

Then one day I noticed something else more far-reaching and remarkable about the small dog with the "human brain," as the breed is often characterized. On days when the pain in my body was a ten and training time was impossible, and I was barely cogent or living, Foster Logan Potts would draw near to me. His special magic was grace personified. He always knew when I was at my worst. He always knew exactly where to place his body next to mine. Foster always knew my need and devoted himself to my comfort.

My pain always lessened, and I felt better. Better yet, I felt loved and supported, and I didn't have to ask. The bond between us had become unspoken in a way that was not visible to the naked eye. Foster was one of the most amazing gifts that came out of my daughter's uniquely perceptive desire to help her suffering mother.

I could rely on Foster to be there for me and to relieve my pain, and so could Sylver. Interestingly enough, he kept very safe and spacious boundaries otherwise. That is, when I was just my usual 7 or 8 level pain or maybe even 5 or 6, he would be close but not touching. When I screamed, he came in closer to subdue my rage. When I was feeling good for me, it was easy to see that Foster was feeling good, too.

In some ways, I felt it a disservice to such a young pet, but most of the time I knew the Creator had sent me a very gifted healer who could change my life. It did make Foster a little possessive. I don't know if Foster ever forgave me for bringing the girls, his life companions in later years. Ultimately though, I believe his life was extended and so much the better for having a family of his own species to possess, protect and love.

Foster was the epitome of health. He was almost never sick. He was strong and limber for his size and could jump very high in the air. I exercised his hind legs as a regular part of his daily regimen. He even sat by my feet at the piano when I played. He snuggled close to the pedals to resonate with the vibrations, a place of honor he relinquished over time. But always faithful, my little piece of God, reminded me of a wonderful Creator who made us all.

Foster Logan Potts was actually one of my very first effective alternative therapies. He was my first naturopath. He predated energy medicine, supplements, regimen and recovery. At that time, life was relapse after relapse and mountains of prescriptions and diagnoses and crippling, alienating experiences. All but for Foster, and, of course, Sylver, the facilitator of all my hopes, these were very dark days.

When I was divorced and unemployed and feeling alone and worthless, Foster saved the day and created an opening for healing light. Day in and day out, we trained. We tried again and again to find a way out of the abyss of rejection, misunderstanding and abuse. The vicious cycle had taken its toll and I was lost and broken. He was whole and willing. I was blessed.

My poetic tribute to Foster is an all-time favorite. The closing verse of *Foster Knows* says:

Foster knows

For sure he does.

He hears and sniffs

Through all the stuff.
He comes with a special gift
Of being pure, unbounded love.

For seven years, Foster was my only doggie healer. My loyal companion nurtured my spirit and spiced up my days with laughter. Whether jumping for his favorite treats, licking a chewy into oblivion or signaling a caller at the door with precision and predictability, he could ease the pain of my fallen soul. These were great feats for a mere 15 pounds of pure, unconditional love. Always fervently by my side, handsome and proud to be purposeful, loved and needed for his time here, Foster could say more than most humans with a look or even a rare lick. He was the advocate of my life's cause. By the way, Foster was my father's middle name.

And then there were two.

Foster takes a wife: Aria Rose

About five years into my staunch and stoic healing process, another earth-shattering disaster struck my life with my precious daughter. The Flagler River we called it. The inner city flood of 2001 in Washington, D.C., was just 30 days prior to 9-11. The long and short of it is that Sylver and I were almost electrocuted. Our lives were thrown off course, to put it mildly. Or, at least, that is one interpretation.

The miraculous rescue that I had carried out with the help of the angels and, perhaps, my spirit guide was still more than we could fathom even though we had lived through it.

Sylver had been trapped in the basement during the turbulent storm that disabled our house. She was standing on the floor in a T-shirt going into panic by the time I reached the front door that was swollen and stuck. I had to literally tear the door off to rescue her from the dirty, gushing water.

The power of the hour was the 40-year-old hammer that I used to strike open the door. This "ol' hammer" that I always kept in my home was the first one I ever owned when we lived in South Carolina. I brought it to D.C. when we moved in 1976.

God was all around us for sure. I knew that some "other forces" assisted me to carry out the rescue. I felt "carried" down the hall from my bedroom as I calmly raced to get to the basement. I knew I had help. I could feel it!

For just a short while, I had the superhuman strength of a mother's devotion to her child. The experience was nonetheless devastating. Sylver and I would be struggling for months to rise up again.

We found ourselves deeply immersed in the master classes of earth school, in the most literal sense, scooping the dirty water out of our shoes and cars. Sylver's basement apartment in our home at 2030 Flagler Street, NW, was "sewerized" in a twinkling by colliding rainstorms that overloaded the drainage system in our neighborhood. All her possessions were tossed and floating around our feet in murky water just at our knees.

It was August 11, 2001; I'll never forget it in this lifetime. It was the day after my 52nd birthday.

As fate would have it, I had been rejoicing on most days in 2001 in thanksgiving for the amazing results of several years of intense therapies and regimens. I was praising God for blessings and more blessings. I was feeling well again beyond my highest hopes.

The Flagler Flood would bring an abrupt end to my celebration of healing.

Pain and trauma came back into my life with indescribable force. This triggered yet another emotional illness. I was diagnosed with a classic case of post-traumatic stress disorder (PTSD) as part of the impact on my health of the flood of 8-11. A new treatment plan would be essential so that all the progress I had gained would not be lost again, perhaps forever this time.

Fortunately, for about six years energy medicine had become my greatest healing resource. I had many resources and healing helpers. Tom to the rescue! Craniosacral therapy, Peter Levine and years of study paid off big time. Three months later in December, I was no longer flailing under water in my dreams having flashbacks of the tragedy and injuries of 8-11 due to the Flagler Flood. A series of trauma therapy sessions gradually dissipated the disturbing post traumatic stress syndrome nightmares.

Thirty days after our date with 8-11, it was 9-11-2001. The Flagler Flood was simply not to be compared to a terrorist attack in the U.S. I thought it was totally conceivable we might declare war and thousands more would die. That overrode a minor flood on my street in the nation's capital any day.

But our D-day had already happened. We were picking up the pieces, and there was much work to be done to regain our equilibrium and prosper. This was a tall order for two fragile Southern belles. We were walking in darkness like the night. And morning did come.

It was Christmas again. While I was feeling better and recovering well from the added burden of PTSD, I was still battling depression and dysthymia with all I could muster and all that I had learned. My snail's pace recovery was just not enough for Sylver who realized that I was still suffering deeply and needed another jolt to my rehabilitation strategies.

So Sylver and her new boyfriend, Daryl, decided that another doggie was the answer to my prayers for healing. They would get a wife for Foster and a new puppy for Mommie to love.

Aria Rose was perhaps the cutest puppy I had ever seen. She was tiny and had the pointy ears that Schnauzers are known for. She was a puppy with a hairdo, for goodness sake! I had never seen a puppy that was coiffed. Her bottom layer of hair fell in a short flip around her silky torso. I fell in love with her instantly! She slept on my neck her first night with us.

All was good again. There is no magic like puppy magic. And I had the cutest puppy ever. What more could I ask? She was spirited and loving and a joy to behold.

I thought for an instant that Sylver and Daryl were surely crazy. We had just lost so much. How could we afford another mouth to feed, doggie or otherwise? In the subsequent instance, I knew it was okay. God would take care of us.

How could I refuse such a touching act from my beloved Sylver? She knew I needed help, and she did something about it. I have her to thank for all my wonderful doggie experiences, lessons and stories. They are many and endless and treasures for all time.

Aria Rose was my new magnificent obsession. She was so sweet and cuddly, a very girly doggie. She was named Aria in tribute to my favorite musical genre, opera. She was named Rose in honor of my mother. Of course, she and Foster had to be named for my mom and dad.

Aria loved Foster and tried to play with him all day long. Foster would have no part of her in the beginning. Yet, she never gave up on him. I learned so much from watching her continually seek Foster's attention only for him to growl and send her running and jumping all over the furniture. Aria or MuuMuu, as she came to prefer to be called, taught me once again the greatest doggie lesson of all, the power of unconditional love. (My poem in her honor is appropriately titled, *MuuMuu Loves*.) She would ultimately teach Foster about the doggie birds and bees and become the mother of his progeny—all girls!

As circumstances would have it, Aria Rose would not get the same training as Foster. She was smart and learned a few tricks as a small pup. Our lives were so topsy-turvy after the flood that there was little time for doggie lessons beyond potty training.

Aria's very special role in our lives was to make us feel loved. She needed no training in lovingness. She was a natural.

Three months later we were moving again because our house was slowly deteriorating from the damage caused by the floodwaters. Mice and squirrels and bacteria were invading our space with a vengeance. I was getting sick again and had a relapse and many physical challenges. My sympathetic side (left side), the side that I had rescued Sylver with, was finally screaming out in protest against the extreme trauma to the muscles in my arm from the hammering on the waterbound basement door trapping Sylver.

For two weeks in January 2002, I could barely move except from bed to couch to bed, the pain in my upper body was so intense. While Sylver was traveling to help pay the rent, my nieces, Dianna and Dana, attended to my meals and the dog walking. I took pain meds, resumed therapies and prayed for deliverance. I had come so far and was doing so much better. Why did I have to fall again? And again? And again?

Meanwhile, Aria Rose and my beloved Foster kept me smiling and laughing through all the pain and darkness and uncertainty. Who knew that one day they would expand my doggie world beyond my wildest dreams?

And then there were seven!

Foster becomes a dad:
Blanche and the brood are born

It is a well-known country code that you never leave females in heat alone for a second around potential sires. Yes? Yes! Well, I knew this well having grown up on country roads in rural South Carolina. But I guess I lost my touch for such things as a city girl. And that is how it happened. We looked the other way, and the rest is history.

We had been in our new house on Gallatin Street for about five months when MuuMuu was having her first heat. Like responsible dog owners, we had separated her and Foster because, of course, we

113

knew they were not neutered. We always dreamed of mating Foster, but we wanted to wait until Aria's second heat.

But MuuMuu and Foster had other plans for us. As it turned out they did know better than we did. The timing they picked was much better than the summer heat we were contemplating. Almost exactly 62 days later (after the day we saw them necking or something), the puppies were born—five in a row. The next chapter in our doggie saga was birthed.

I believe Blanche will one day be a mascot. There is something in her eyes that has called out to the storyteller in me since her early months. Yet I did not follow the impulses when they came, except to make a few notes. I am perhaps waiting for crystallization of the concept to emerge.

In any case, the "Baby Blanche-kins" as I affectionately call her, changed my ideas about doggie souls forever. Just as surely as I write these words, Blanche chose and cultivated her position as the third mini-Schnauzer in our family. Her sacred contract played out brilliantly.

Although I was the midwife at Blanche's birth, I cannot say her birth order for sure. They all looked the same at birth. They were born a half hour apart and cleaned to perfection by their loving mama. The first arrival may have been Blanche. I sometimes feel this way because it was Aria's hardest delivery. Blanche did turn out to be the runt of the litter. But exact birth order is only speculation.

Each pup was perfect, and Aria was the perfect mom. She did not need my help. She just needed me to make a bed and turn off the lights. The latter action I am certain happened much too slowly. Nonetheless, when I finally figured out that she needed to be alone and in the dark, she delivered each pup with awesome intelligence. I was amazed at every special mothering and nurturing event from the first pup to the last.

Blanche was one of five pups born that early Easter morn in

March 2003. They were all girls. Foster had fallen true to the Potts' genetics in fathering girls. It is what Potts' men did best. My father had three girls and my brother had five. My brother was the only boy born into the family.

Five healthy dog girls with Foster's signature stripe down their backs were crawling around in the makeshift doggie bed.

Of course, Foster had no clue about what was happening. He had lived seven years without this particular experience so he was confounded at best. Instinctively, he stayed out of Aria's way. Though I did notice his concern when one escaped the lair when he happened to be visiting. He was comfortable as long as the pups stayed in one place. Schnauzers are like that about most things. There is a little control freak in each and every one of them! Foster was no exception. But he was cool. Mostly, he stayed out of trouble.

So I guess you are wondering where we got the name Blanche? Another long story? Of course.

For identification purposes, all the puppies needed names. Humans need labels to organize matter. So names were assigned with the idea that they one day might change.

The leader of the pack who would also become the largest was the first to be named. She was called Edith, a homespun alias for Sylver's best friend, Angel, who was visiting us at the time of their birth.

Edith, who would later be named, Sonata, in keeping with our love of music, joined the family of Daryl's sister, Zaria, and lives in Kentucky these days.

The next in line in size and presence was Renee. Her name was selected to honor my Goddaughter of the same name.

Renee, the pup, would become a member of the family of Gerado and Heather Velez. She would be renamed, Stella Bella Diva. How's that for a tag! In 2014, Stella is an official service dog basking in the beauty of Hawaii. Aloha, Stella!

Then there was Piffy, nickname for Epiphany, the only name that would remain unchanged by new owners. Epiphany had a special halo that made her appear to be always mediating. She was deemed the spiritual one hence her light-filled name.

Piffy went to live with the Mitchel's pretty close by in Virginia. She had a life of luxury—a car seat, fur bed and a big yard of her own. She also had an internal sensing device in case she became lost, a very 21st century girl. What a life! Piffy joined Foster in heaven in 2010.

Piffy shared very similar coloring and markings with the next to last of the clan, so we decided to label them twins and give them matching names, Epiphany and Stephanie. The two of them usually lined up side by side and ate together as well. Somehow, all the pups understood the natural pecking order.

Stephanie was purchased by a couple who lived in New York City. So we traveled in our trusty Jeep to the Big Apple to deliver her to her new owners. Her new name was Schyla. The husband of the couple was a dog trainer so she surely made out not too shabby.

That brings us back to Blanche, the baby of the lot, and a precocious pup the likes of which I never encountered in any of my prior experiences with pets. Somehow mysteriously, Blanche would not grow as fast as the others. She was significantly smaller and seemed to know that it was a privileged position to hold. I believe she manifested an intention that we held in our hearts with great hope and faith.

Sylver and I had fantasized often about breeding a micro-Schnauzer or toy-size offspring. We noticed that Foster, though well built and exceptionally smart, was smaller than most other miniature Schnauzers that we saw over the years. Aria also turned out to be smaller than normal. We were often asked how we managed to get two small ones. They chose us, according to Sylver's account of their selection. So it was just divinity at work again.

It was often my fervent prayer throughout Aria's pregnancy that

116

the puppies would be healthy and small. My therapist, Michele, had often referred to our dogs as our "gold mine." She, too, held the vision. It was Michele that labeled them, micro-Schnauzers. Imagine if we could develop a toy breed!

Well, somewhere along the line, Blanche heard our prayers and sensed our imaginings. For all of a sudden, she was a micro, small and sweet and special, a dream come true. She took her place as "the least of them" with great pride and became the best. It was not long before she held an irrevocable place in our hearts and lives, well maneuvered and strategized.

Blanche would remain a petite eight pounds until the age of four while her sisters continued to grow bigger. At first, she was not a foodie. I never quite understood a dog that did not like to eat. Conveniently, she gave up her modest diet once she had secured her place in our home. Her love affair with food would come much later and fatten her up a bit. In 2014, at eleven years old, she is a foodie who dances for any crumbs that come close to her nose. There is more!

As Blanche grew smarter and cuter, the rough and tumble of her sisters was a bit much so she found a way to be alone with me whenever she could. When it was time to come into my bedroom for petting and picking up, Blanche always waited to come last after the other four had their turn and left the room. There was no competition for her petting time. She got to stay on the bed with the master mom much longer than the others. Even though her sisters made their way to wonderful new homes, Blanche was stuck like glue to me.

As long as I live I will probably never see such a clever trick from a dog. It reminds me of the antics of my siblings more than of any other puppies I knew. She had a human lilt in her eyes that was almost eerie. She was peaceful and calm most of the time and had an uncanny air of confidence, for a dog, no less a puppy.

Blanche barked only when her food was threatened and usually ate alone. A disadvantage of being the smallest and most laid back, the sisters would eat most of the food before she started. Not in a rush to partake of her portion, she had to employ extreme tactics to secure her bowl long enough to finish a meal. It was the only time that I knew Blanche could growl. Otherwise, she was just peace personified with no worldly complaint that was yet detectable.

Blanche knew she was special and understood her soul's journey perfectly well. As I have not told you the most important relationship to her naming process, let me clarify. Blanche was named for Sylver; I know once again you are confused. How could you get Blanche out of Sylver? Again a parallel personality takes the credit.

A family predisposed to assigning names to otherwise unacceptable aspects of our personalities, Sylver and Angel and I were given to choosing "alter" names for ourselves on occasion. I know it sounds crazy, but it was all in fun.

The name, Blanche, originated with the character Blanche Devereaux, played expertly by Rue McClanahan in the television series, *The Golden Girls*. Blanche was sassy and sultry and oh so sexy and coy. Sylver was given the nickname, Blanche, as a teaser by Angel and me for a role she played in high school. The bad girl, Cookie, was a prostitute in a modernized version of the play, *God's Trombones*. The girl who had to act like a sex kitten on demand was Sylver's most popular "alter name" amongst us girls. So Cookie was renamed Blanche. Both ladies wore the names well. Since one of the pups had to be named for Sylver, it seemed that the sweet little one was the likely candidate. And so it is.

Now it should be abundantly clear why Blanche is the one that stayed. How could Sylver bear to part with her very own namesake? Blanche became the one to keep.

Blanche sits securely on the throne of entitlement and wears her presence in peace and harmony, an example to us all.

I wrote a poem about Blanche in 2006, entitled *Baby Blanchekins*. The second verse describes her soul's journey best:

Baby Blanche-kins,
Smallest of five;
Knew how to take advantage
Of her size.
Awfully smart for one so small;
She knew just how to get it all.
Attention, that is,
From all the rest.
Of her sisterly brood,
She is surely the best.

Singing is one family trait Blanche seems not to have inherited. Her bark sounds pretty much like the squealing of a stuck pig and zings your ears if you are not aware. I am patient with this one fault due to her feeble attempts to bark above the pitch of her mom, a sparkling "coloratura." MuuMuu has always had a melodious timbre to her bark while Foster's was intimidating and a little pitchy. Blanche could not seem to find a tone to compete with her mom's, so she just wails feverously. One thing I will say in her behalf is that she is definitely heard when she speaks.

The doggies never cease to amaze and continually teach me about life in ways no human could begin to understand had they not the experience of such as well. I honor and revere their presence in my life. Notwithstanding their unconditional love, which is common knowledge to most, they are teachers of great life lessons and my favorite "pieces of God."

They give so much and it is an honor to be able to return a bit of their unconditional love when I can.

One of my best examples of their special understanding of life experiences is once again rooted in energy medicine. I, of course, apply "healing hands" to my doggies whenever the need arises. I have brought Aria back from the brink of death, but that is another story.

Here is the learning from that experience: Dogs know when they need help and when they don't. Or it could be that they know when they will and when they won't. In either case, whenever I apply a craniosacral hold to their bodies, they respond very quickly or not at all.

From my several years of observations, they (all three of them) embrace and sit quietly in the hold pattern when they are feeling really ill. I have used the parasympathetic contacts to contain them when frightened or shaking. Ninety-nine percent of the time, it has calmed them. There is seldom residual observable stress after these sessions. And somehow I always sense their gratitude for the return to balance.

Every time I hold them with a healing intention, I recognize just how much alike are all God's creatures. I feel the Breath of Life within my doggies as clearly as I feel it within my homo sapien clients. It is the same Intelligence and the same Source!

I am grateful for this teaching from my hairy friends. They add so much to my life all the while making me laugh with their very special antics and making me cry when they cry. I will share my being with them always and forever. Thanks be to God!

I have written several poetic tributes inspired by my beloved doggies. The closing verse in my poem, *I Luv My Doggies,* expresses our love affair best:

I luv my doggies,
Close to my heart,
Saying,
I am here.
I am love.
I luv you too! Arf!

CHAPTER 8

What Worked, Part 1: Supplements

T HE MANIFESTATIONS OF THINGS THAT WORKED to heal my dis-eases all started in 1992 with a product called Km and a sister-friend, Phillipa Brisbane. I do not recall the specific reason Phil, as we called her, was taking and selling Km. There had to be a good reason though. She was a reasonable sort and even a somewhat skeptical personality not given to hoaxes.

Phil was a close part of my personal life in her role as manager of my daughter's budding vocal career. She was one of Sylver's best experiences with manager types, and we regarded her as family. Phil's work with Sylver would subsequently lead to my daughter's job as a regular background singer for and protégé of jazz and pop singer Jean Carne. Jean is still a close friend and someone we love dearly. So needless to say, Phil and I were very close and had high regard for each other's instincts.

The day would come when Phil would bring me a mineral food supplement in a white bottle with orange letters, labeled Km. Well, what do you know, I needed the ingredients in Km—especially potassium and magnesium—or so I found out. A brown liquid preparation containing 14 synergistic herbs, this magic potion #1 had the power to heal. Almost at once, I started to feel better and had noticeably more energy. Km was not so savory to the taste.

I learned a great healing lesson, that I could drink anything if I knew it would help me, nasty or not. Maybe this was my first alter personality. It is truly incredible that a sugar addict like me ended up gulping down the nasties for any purpose.

Nonetheless, Km became a regular part of my daily diet and the first supplement to address the mineral imbalances associated with fibromyalgia. I took it faithfully twice daily. It kept hope alive.

Whatever the secret formula was, Km worked for me. It was all that mattered in a world of toxic meds that just did not do the job and that yielded unending side effects. I took my relief wherever I found it and trusted when Spirit so directed me. Km was my friend for five or six years before I moved on to other potions and treatments. It did not matter to me what others thought about supplements. My *knowing self* was in charge.

Phillipa's introduction to Km led to a new pattern in my life. Trusting the universe to send my Spirit the next best thing and allowing my instincts to choose wisely was the advent of my sacred contract with healing. My initiation was some sort of *spiritual muscle testing* that blossomed like a flower. I will say more about this gift of discernment that keeps me aligned with my purpose and my passions in Chapter 10.

For the most part (and I don't recommend it), I did very little research into ingredients in the supplements I chose. My selections were what I call "spiritual choices" 99 percent of the time. In my defense, it was still the time before the Internet, so research was not so easy.

What is more important to illustrate here is that the trail of things that worked for me all started with Phillipa bringing the Km—a humble beginning. Thanks Phil!

Phillipa earned her heavenly angel wings in 2011. I am sad that she is not here to receive her credit for initiating my path of supplements that worked. However, I am certain that she watches over me. Phil may even be in my writing room right now making sure I tell her part of the story right.

Another curious pattern also emerged from my track record with Km. No matter how many distributorships I owned, I was seldom a good salesperson. I did very poorly as a Km seller.

Most folks did not believe there was anything wrong with me anyway. So I was not very convincing. Supplements were not very accepted in the early '90s. Fibromyalgia—what is that, for goodness sakes?

I was just crazy Paula. You never know what she is going to come up with. The best news here is that it just did not matter that I could not sell Km. I made great strides with self-healing methods from that point forward whether people believed me or not. Now they do!

I did not realize at the time, of course, the significance of the Km story. So many new beginnings are vested in this recapitulation. I would also become very organized around "what I know works" and almost never missed a dose. My regularity, I am sure made a difference. It was a valuable trait that I would benefit from for many years to come.

The lavender signature

I was a girl of many fragrances in my early youth. (I am now in my later youth.) A single scent never did seem to satisfy me. So there was Opium, Halston, Norrel and many others to enchant my soul and keep me sweet. I prefer robust, romantic scents and perfumes mostly. I am surely not a toilet water girl.

Anyway, one Christmas day, my neighborhood friend, Rhonald Angelo, gave me some Crabtree and Evelyn's liquid lavender bath soap. And the rest, as they say, is history. My first use of this soap was the beginning of a new signature therapy in my life. Lavender oil soon became my new favorite thing. It made me feel better. The first time I took a shower with it, I had a relaxation response. Relief in a bottle of soap—who knew?

I remember quite vividly sensing my muscles let go and even rejuvenate a little from my first shower with the relaxing lavender soap. I suspected I was really crazy! I don't remember how long it took me to share what was happening. I just kept on doing what made me feel better. I trusted the feel-better part.

My first lavender shower was a significant breakthrough that would remain among my most efficient therapies. In 2014, I still take lavender baths regularly. I am never far away from a bottle of lavender oil. My relationship with essential oils grew in leaps and bounds over my fifteen-year intense healing period. I will sing their praises ceaselessly.

Lavender oil became a personal signature in both my everyday life and my life as a healing arts practitioner. Shades of lavender and purple adorn my treatment room, bedroom and wardrobe.

There is almost no use of this most gentle of substances that eluded me. I sprinkled it on my pillow at night and restored my sleep.

I gashed my foot at the beach and poured it neat into the wound and completely healed the injury with no scar. It never got infected, and I never used anything else on it—except sterile water.

My sister, Camille, with whom I was beaching that day was a witness. By then, she was aware that I traveled with my trusty bottle of lavender. I inhaled it for sinus congestion and headaches and most often got relief. Talk about magic potion, it was and still is the best single essential oil I know.

The shower experience was in the '90s. It is now 2014, and I still regularly use essential oils and blended oils of all kinds, including master oils and chakra oils. Of course, now, essential oils are in everything from baby products to dish soap. My pioneer spirit rides again!

I can rejoice for another, "I told you so" moment for justPaula, you know, the crazy girl. I love it! I love it! I love it! I thank God for these blessed substances, the Breath of Life at its best!

I am seldom without frankincense, tea tree and another favorite flower essence, Rescue Remedy. You will probably find all of these in my purse on any given day. These sacred substances are among my most reliable natural healing resources. Resources are energies that support and restore body balance where and when depleted or blocked.

Essential oils give the body oxygen and vibrational frequencies that alter chemistry and even DNA. I once read that oils do not kill bacteria but provide an environment where they cannot grow.

Young Living Oil Company developed an oil blend called "Thieves," which purports to have this no-growth effect. It is based on a formulation used by grave robbers during the Black Plague in medieval times. I carry a bottle of the Thieves spray in my purse and keep extras close by to ward off airborne toxicities.

The power of essences is limitless in my world. I have used them to move bone and tissue and with breathwork to reduce both anxiety and pain. I have used essential oils directly applied to the skin, in poultice packs, in raindrop therapy for spinal adjustments, and just about anywhere else you can imagine. I have also used oils internally, although there are those who would argue against it. A few drops of peppermint oil in my morning tea are my latest application for a happy tummy.

Oh, and lavender repels fleas, too, so my doggies get a few drops in their bath. The dogs also wear a little cedarwood from time to time as their special perfume. My love affair with essential oils should be pretty clear by now!

The green applesauce saga

Thank you, sister Tracie Rose! Now here is a friend that I can truly thank for many things. She always comes to visit with presents, the most fragrant oils and just plain ol' good vibes. I call her my spirit sister. Tracie is one of those people who brings people together. She has good instincts and is very meticulous and discerning about what she puts in her body.

In any case, it was Tracie Rose who brought me the concoction that is fondly called "green applesauce" by everyone in my family—a dark green powder mixed into a big jar of applesauce.

Before this auspicious day, I had yet another tragic episode with my medical conditions. I called upon Tracie's spiritual guidance to refer me to someone who could tell me something. I was bedridden with pain and feeling the adverse effects of overmedication like a lion roaring in my soul.

I was desperate for help, an unfortunately well-known state for a panic disorder sufferer. Tracie referred me to her spirit-sister, Imani. Once again, a monumental milestone in my healing history was in the making.

Imani was an anointed healer who came on the wings of God's love for me. A clairvoyant nutritionist, Imani's second sight was a powerful resource. She told me in no uncertain terms that I was poisoning myself with medications. She was sure that I was lingering dangerously in the Valley of the Shadow of Death and needed a way out. Ironically, she gave these revelations to me just as I was having the same thoughts in my own head. It was an overwhelming synchronicity.

Earlier on that very same day, I had an epiphany in my spirit that said, "Get off the meds or kill yourself!" Notice the semantic nuance. The voice inside my knowing did not say "die." It said, "Kill yourself." It may not be an obvious distinction to you, but my knowing self understood that I needed to feel responsible.

This holy moment was an instructive metaphor for my resistance to healing. I was, indeed, the culprit. It was I who was killing myself, however slowly. Imagine having that thought. Now, imagine having that thought and believing it!

A rush of empowerment came upon me. I was blessed beyond measure by the insightful wisdom that brought Light and green applesauce. Now I got it! I would have to stop contributing to my own demise. I would have to stop killing myself.

Imani asked if I was familiar with blue green algae and put me in touch with a particular brand. I committed to starting a program of detoxification of my medications immediately. The side effects had become overbearing by then anyway. The blurred vision was getting so much worse. Antidepressants were known for this side effect, among many others.

Before I could order the algae, Tracie Rose came to the rescue. Yet another date with destiny was upon me. Tracie came to visit one day and brought a gallon jar of applesauce spiked with blue green algae.

How could she have known to do that? Surely divinity was at work here. That was 1994. Today, almost 20 years later, I am still consuming copious amounts of green applesauce on a regular basis. Superfood, like spirulina, is commonly known today. It is all over the place and in most health food stores.

Right away, I established a detox regimen with the blue green algae. I used it to help wean myself off all my meds, starting with the antidepressants. I took it slow and it worked.

For the record, blue green algae tasted nasty, so applesauce made it palatable. I also took algae in juice and water, if necessary. I have mixed it in yogurt and smoothies as well. Of course, in 2014, superfood is everywhere as are all kinds of health drinks for energy. Odwalla is my fallback green food tonic when I am not mixing my own favorite brand, *Green Vibrance*.

I will say it again. Superfood! Strictly food for thought. Be sure to consult your physician. Consider the value of your own personal experience as you investigate the healing modalities that are right for you. I have a master's degree in educational research, so I speak research.

As of this writing, I am pharmaceutical free on a regular basis. I do, however, keep Ativan on hand for rare emergencies and acute situations.

For the record, I am not anti-medication. Let me say it again. I am not anti-medication. I am, however, anti-over-medication. And that is the condition I was in when all this happened.

In addition to detoxing the meds, I taught myself to manage my pain and physical challenges on a regular basis with diet, supplements, exercise, breathwork and energy work. The latter I do myself or get from my cadre of caring practitioners to whom I have regular access.

I am not suggesting that I did the detox program with green applesauce alone. I also learned how to juice and followed a very specific power regimen daily. I received effective weekly sessions with my myotherapist. Ten years later, the combination restored me to health and physical functioning in ways that still take my breath away. I added energy medicine studies during this time as well. My course of therapy was my full-time occupation.

Pioneering is hard work. When you don't know where you are going, you don't know when you are going to get there. Intuitively, I followed my internal healer with great precision.

Cell salts to the rescue

Speaking of remedies that rescue, cell salts did just that with miraculous results on more than one occasion. Cell salts had a direct line to my heart. A sublingual delivery system has always been the most comfortable and compatible with my sensitive digestion.

My history of anemia and B-12 shots (more shots!) as a young adult sent me on a quest for a better way to absorb these vital nutrients when I became ill in my forties. I searched high and low for the best sublingual B vitamins I could find early in my healing process. For me, a B vitamin deficiency was an obvious diagnosis considering my problems with muscles, mood and energy.

My serious dietary changes including adding lots of dark green leafy veggies, green applesauce and juicing fruits and vegetables ultimately led to less reliance on specific vitamin supplements. It wasn't long before I strayed away from the sublingual B, which was good because it got harder to find.

The advent of cell salts in my arsenal of supplements that worked was yet another benefit of my work with Tom Langan and Somatic Energy Therapies, www.setherapies.org. Tom and his partner, Dr. Johnny Henderson, recommended that I try cell salts to address mineral deficiencies, potassium (remember Km?) and magnesium in particular.

It was love at first dose! My muscles responded instantaneously to taking cell salts. This was Big! Cell salts restored my flexibility and reduced the pain in my muscles. The response to cell salts in my system was uplifting to my spirits. My training in energy medicine prepared me to tune in to the noticeable and sometimes visible physical effects of imbibing cell salts.

Of course, mineral imbalances have long been associated with symptoms of fibromyalgia as well as many other illnesses—like heart disease. However, my challenge was always about how to get the minerals in my system without adversely impacting my digestion. The sublingually administered cell salts were the perfect solution!

So now that I have piqued your interest, here is the scoop on these magical supplements: Cell salts are homeopathic preparations of the minerals that are the building blocks of our bodies, according to the website, *Healing 4 Soul.* Adsorbed through saliva, cell salts are reported to improve assimilation and utilization of these vital mineral nutrients. They support proper cell function to optimize health and ameliorate physical and emotional symptoms, such as anxiety, mood swings, pain and digestive problems. Minerals—potassium, calcium, magnesium and many more—are the foundation for many bodily functions including enzyme activity in the body. They serve as catalysts in energy cycles and functions.

Medical doctors and naturopaths have proved the effectiveness of cell salts for over two hundred years. Like most supplements, there is also considerable controversy about their use. In my world, they are another example of remedies that work.

About two years ago, I started having back pain and stiffness and tight muscles, which were resistant to stretching or lengthening. At first, I decided that "old age" was creeping in. Oh, no!

When I came to my senses after the initial fear response, I took a minute to reflect on potential causes. My playback revealed that I had been derelict in my mineral duty for over a year. I was magnesium deficient again. Bad Paula! All this healing work does get to be a bit much at times—not to mention costly!

Help was not far away. A call to Tom and Johnny would bring my physical miseries and regimen slippages back into harmony and balance.

As soon as I took my first dose, the cell salts played a symphony of relief in my fascia. Like a soft, silky breeze I could feel the internal reorganization in my tissues. My chemical connection to the Health Within was recharged and ready to move.

I could perform back bends and squats on the exercise ball without strain or injury. I could ride my stationary bike and stretch and jump for joy. JustPaula was back on the dance floor!

So I send many thanks to Tom and Johnny—my ever-vigilant stewards of what's new—for keeping me in sync with my mineral needs. Better yet, big hugs for constantly expanding my horizons and my view of life beyond the veil.

To close out this section, I say in summation that supplements work. There are many skeptics and naysayers. It is okay. Doubters help to keep me honest and sometimes safer. Unbelievers help me work a little harder to speak with confidence and conviction and, at least, clues that help validate my results, conclusions and claims of attribution. The polarity of opposites is useful in the process of reliable discernment with reasonable certainty.

Consult your physicians and holistic practitioners—both—before using supplements. Perhaps a little muscle testing will help!

CHAPTER 9

What Worked, Part 2:
Therapies and Therapeutic Ideas

W HEN I SAT DOWN TO REWRITE THIS SECTION of the chapter on *what worked,* I soon realized that I was in the middle of a "full circle" moment. Aha! God is, indeed, bigger!

SynergyDance

My research on SynergyDance to ensure that I got it right brought forth an illuminating catharsis that was clearly divinely ordered. Reading Charmaine's bio and viewing her videos online engendered deep emotion about how far I truly have come from where I started. Spontaneously, I got up from my writing station to exhale and receive the Breath of Life that was palpable in my whole self. I felt like I was breathed by God!

SynergyDance and originator, Charmaine Lee, were my launching pad for my sacred contract with energy healing. Without a doubt, my magnificent metamorphosis started in a dance class. I have said this several times by now. This fact will always be worth repeating.

Most of what I will say to describe SynergyDance I excerpted directly from the website article dated August 8, 2011—www .Synergy Dance.com. I could not have said it better. Here is a concise explanation:

> SynergyDance is designed to involve the body, mind and emotions in movement (or "deep play") as scientist and Molecules of Emotion author, Candace Pert, has called it. Drawing structure from the energy medicine systems of polarity therapy, Synergy Dance is a hybrid of Indian yogic tradition, Eastern martial and healing arts and Western holistic approaches to personal wellness. SynergyDance also incorporates world dance and music.

SynergyDance is a form of expressive dance that encourages and stimulates inner exploration into the biodynamics of the human soul and its relationship to the physical body and life experience. There is no doubt in my mind whatsoever that SynergyDance saved my life.

A native of South Africa, my friend and SynergyDance instructor Charmaine's sacred contract with healing is as deep as mine, if not more so. Finding therapy in movement that birthed SynergyDance as a primary calling was no small wonder for a talented dancer who was once a refugee with no home to go back to.

A professional ballet soloist in her teens, Charmaine's broad scope of dance studies includes modern, jazz, tap, Spanish, belly dancing, classical Greek, African and more. All her classes reflected her embodiment of these dance forms and her unique ability to transform each movement into an opportunity for healing.

Polarity therapy precepts and principles were introduced to my body, mind and spirit every time I danced through a new routine. The five elemental principles of polarity therapy as qualities of energy movement—earth, water, fire, air and ether—were integrated into my felt sense of the Health Within. The idea of an intrinsic life force became real.

In truth, there was very little routine in SynergyDance movements in the classical sense. At its best, the fluidity of the forms and intentions generated a more balanced flow in the energy systems in my body, effortlessly. This was something I could feel that had textures and sensations that made me noticeably better in my body, mind and spirit.

Of course, I did not understand a lot about the tenets of energy healing for months and months. Once again, I trusted the "feel better" part. I also trusted my inner guidance system that sent me the very compelling command to, just do it!

Even when I could do only half a class because of the pain, I'd sit and watch other dancers keep on going. But I always went back to try again. Even when I flared up after class and had to be still for days to recover, I soaked in my lavender baths and returned to class. Even when it hurt like hell, when I finally made it through the entire class routine, I rejoiced! My warrior spirit kept me going until I could do three classes a week and not end up flat on my back. This was truly God's redemptive grace and mercy.

SynergyDance worked! As I practiced weekly and sometimes daily at home, the pain and disability melted away like butter on summer corn. Healing miracles moved through every muscle, bone and sinew. I could dance again! I could soon walk without a cane. Dr. Doubt It was headed for the showers—and I don't mean Gatorade or champagne either. SynergyDance was my saving grace and my healing champion.

SynergyDance and Charmaine have been featured in the books, *Everything You Need to Know to Feel Go(o)d* by Candace Pert and *Magic at Work* by Carol Pearson, as well as in *The Washington Post,* and *Pathways* magazine and on TV and radio.

An enlightening quotation from her website bio is quite informative. Charmaine expresses the gist of healing energy movement very well when she says:

After studying polarity, it is clear that if you focus on the physical, you're focusing on the effect. If you are working with the life force on balancing the mental, emotional and physical, then you are getting at the cause.

All I can say is, "Amen!"

Speaking of polarity, I shared in earlier chapters that Charmaine was also my first polarity therapist. My sessions with her were my leading experiences of energy bodywork. Charmaine's treatment table is also where I would unveil my tendency to dissociate.

This uniquely gifted movement Goddess directed my path to the future when she recommended that I choose Roger Gilchrist as my polarity therapy teacher. She encouraged me to take his very next course and to attend an upcoming seminar at her studio. The rest is . . . you know the answer.

Serendipity, synchronicity and my sacred contract were in perfect alignment. Again, I say, *God Is Bigger!*

I almost forgot that SynergyDance class is also where I met my next healing arts practitioner, Michele. Our story of lovingness that heals appropriately follows next.

Myotherapy: Michele the Miraculous

Now, I am going to get technical and tell you about myotherapy, a form of bodywork that was developed specifically to relieve painful muscles, in particular, trigger-points. This type of muscle therapy is about as specific as it gets to the treatment of fibromyalgia/myofascial trigger-point syndrome complex.

I really do not understand why more people do not know about it or get to benefit from it. Myotherapy was my daily dose of freedom for ten years, and it was covered by my insurance. Thank you, Jesus!

I met Michele Macomber in a SynergyDance class where she was an instructor. She and head teacher, Charmaine, were good friends, and Michele worked in the Synergy business office. We became fast friends and dance buddies. She was training as a polarity therapist and as a Synergy teacher so she understood the application of the principles well. She was also training as a myotherapist.

I had recently heard about myotherapy from a fellow fibromyalgia sufferer with whom I shared a doctor of physiatry. She spoke of it as something that relieved her pain so I remembered the relief part and remained curious.

When Michele told me about her training as a myotherapist, I thought, "What are the chances I would find my therapist in a dance class?"

A dancer would understand me better than anybody. Certainly, I have hit the jackpot! This must be of God! I will ask the powers that be!

I explained to my earth angel, Dr. Adams, what I wanted to do. He prepared the necessary paperwork. As destiny would bear out, my request for this treatment modality was approved.

There was something I could do about the pain. There was something designed to help someone just like me. Somehow I knew this was it. Myotherapy would become the fulcrum of all my healing experiences for the next decade.

Fortunately for me, Michele's treatment was the perfect segue from my program with Dr. Reynolds, my senior practitioner and primary recommending specialist for most of my early years as a patient. Every treatment request required the sanction of a specialist qualified to say that the modality was applicable to my medical condition.

Dr. Reynolds was willing to give me any opportunity that I was willing to fulfill to overcome my pain and disability. He knew how hard I was working. He and Dr. Adams were mentoring every step with support as my medical authorities. They argued my need, and I pioneered the new hope.

It is also no coincidence that Michele was trained from the same texts of Drs. Janet Travel and David Simons for which my Dr. Reynolds served as editor and I as "guinea pig." She was familiar with the technology of trigger-points and trigger-point injections and stretch and spray and all the lingo that I had learned as a patient of Dr. Reynolds. She followed the same principles of frequency and precision in the execution of passive stretch exercises. Amazing grace!

Instead of needles excavating throughout my tissues, points of contact and pressure led the way to relief and rehabilitation. Muscle functions and relationships became primary and perpetuating factors became the enemy to be researched and remedied. Once again, I relearned how to stretch just about every muscle I could name and some I could not even pronounce. I also learned to sense my inner subtle energy movements in ways that expanded my understanding of my body. The relationship between muscle form and function and pain-related dysfunction became inherently visible. I learned to relieve what I could perceive with remarkable accuracy.

The study of *energy medicine* would deepen my experience of anatomical awareness as my years of therapy ensued. My body became a sensory laboratory that I am sure will teach and mystify my spirit for the rest or my life, perhaps beyond.

Michele started her new myotherapy practice in a treatment room housed in the same studio as SynergyDance. I was one of her first patients. My sessions with her would increase to as many as four times a week when I was in the middle of a setback. Our weekly minimum was twice a week.

When I got the hang of it, I did my homework (most of the time) with determination and integrity—fine-tuning every stretch to insure maximum results. Myotherapy worked!

There are no words to describe the benefits I accrued from so many years of regular therapy. It was difficult and demanding, but so worth it. Michele and I operated like a well-oiled machine. She believed in me and I believed in her. We were powerful together. We took my pain apart, muscle-by-muscle, trigger point by trigger point, stretch-by-stretch, hour-by-hour, day-by-day, year by year.

I detoxed meds and took supplements and consulted gurus of all sorts and kept a power regimen going at all times. I learned breath-work and meditation. I took warming, healing baths and ate whole foods and journaled gratitude and affirmations. I sang the Gospel and monitored my thoughts and touched peaks and valleys in my soul's journey that told my whole truth. I watched Oprah's "Change Your Life" series and studied self-help books with a vengeance. Michele's healing touch and natural curiosity and compassion were exactly what I needed to make Health happen.

She was willing to come to the treatment room in my house after leaving her space at the Synergy studio. In the early years, this arrangement was quite convenient and crucial for my healing process. Even when I was at my worst and could not drive, I did not have to miss many sessions. The universe had finally found favor with me.

My treatment room was sanctified by our healing work. With Dr. Travel's *Trigger Point Manuals* close by, we reviewed perpetuating factors and referral patterns with persistence and patience. We learned and relearned muscle names and functions and measured the rise and fall of pain levels on a scale of one to ten. The well-documented manuals of Dr. Travel allowed even me to keep up a bit with Michele's training.

Thanks to early conditioning, I could commit to endless thera-peutic pursuits as though my life depended on it. Indeed, my quality of life was totally dependent on this commitment. I worked around the clock as I taught myself to stretch every 2 hours and to ride an exercise bike to strengthen my legs. I had learned to ride an exercise bike in one of the pain clinics so I was acclimated to the routine.

The dancer in me appreciated the opportunity to move in an

organized manner and was pleased with the prospect of moving my way back to health. I became more and more pain free and more functional as the therapy days passed on. I was less depressed and panicky and more hopeful and even inspired by my own success. I started to experience the true meaning of empowerment long before I would truly understand it.

Oddly enough, this relatively unknown therapy was only the beginning. The early years, restorative myotherapy treatments provided an unexpected course of events and outcomes that amazed me. Michele the Miraculous was at the center of this promising success story. Once again, the student was ready and the teacher came. Michele was one of the primary teachers who came when I was ready to learn new healing alternatives. Even though most folks had no idea what myotherapy was in reality or how it worked, I was the perfect candidate.

True to my pioneer spirit, I was engaged in something unfamiliar and questionable to most people that proved to be remarkable and life changing for me. There was one champion who cared enough to give me her very best, and God did the rest. I was one little candle lighting the way.

Myotherapy is second only to polarity and craniosacral therapies in my catalogue of complementary practices that no one ever heard of. It is still one of the best-kept secrets of my healing process. It was a part of my saving grace. I hope others will find qualified practitioners who can make a difference for them.

Or anyone who reads this book can look up Michele Macomber, MTPT, LMT, online at www.PainFreeMaryland.com.

Polarity therapy: A holistic healer

Destiny had smiled on me and brought me a great teacher in Michele the Miraculous on that landmark date in December 1993. But I did not realize that I was only in kindergarten. I acquired a few rudiments but I needed a holistic paradigm that would redefine my challenges in comprehensive terms. My success as a self-healer and practitioner of wellness depended on this outcome.

So my elementary/secondary teacher appeared in 1995. His name is Roger Gilchrist, founder and CEO of the Wellness Institute of Energetic Studies. He became my mentor, friend, therapist and guidance counselor for my journey to understanding empowerment. A master teacher and a psychotherapist, Roger was uniquely qualified to lead me through an austere healing process with gentleness and compassion.

As the crow flies, SynergyDance led me to Charmaine, who was also a polarity therapist and Charmaine led me to Roger and polarity therapy training. I attended several classes at a two-day seminar and listened to some of the ideas that were being expressed. Although most of the information that was shared made very little sense intellectually that weekend, the bodywork somehow hit home as the right thing to do next.

I made another spiritual choice that felt right and decided to take the next class when it was offered locally. Charmaine recommended that I take Roger's class. It was a match made in heaven!

So now you are asking, "For goodness sakes, what is polarity therapy?"

Here is a brief description:

Polarity therapy had its beginnings in the research, insight and practical applications of Randolph Stone, D.O., D.C., N.D., but its roots are thousands of years older, according to Franklin Sills, dean of the Polarity Therapy Educational Trust in Devon, England.

A native of Austria, Dr. Stone discovered the "missing link" that connects both Eastern and Western thought: energy. He realized that "All life is movement and movement is a manifestation of energy or vital force (Sills)."

From this basic concept, Dr. Stone developed the health-building paradigm called polarity therapy in the 1940s. His central idea, "Energy is the real substance behind the appearance of matter and forms," is every polarity practitioner's mantra.

Often referred to as a healing art, this holistic healing process consists of four interrelated aspects: a system of therapeutic touch, cleansing and health-building diets, special "polarity" exercises and the creation of a positive attitude and lifestyle.

The term "polarity" was selected to describe electromagnetic energy, the idea underlying the ancient health systems of the Orient. Some of us are familiar with Yin and Yang in Chinese philosophy. A *polarity* is a relationship that sets up movement between two opposing poles. The primary objective of polarity therapy is to remove energy blockages and restore balance and harmony to the living system. Whew! That's a lot to absorb!

A.P.P. is the acronym for associate polarity practitioner, which represents the first level of training and credentialing in polarity therapy. I come from a long line of professional students so it was not out of the question for me to engage this educational pursuit.

I did not know where the money was coming from. I never did know, but it always came, and I always made arrangements and agreements in the meantime.

It took the better part of a year and a half to complete all the required sessions and transcriptions of treatment observations. I had the courage of my convictions to keep me inspired to the end.

I struggled through the three weeks of the intensive training program, the hours of practice and the preparation of final reports. I learned about the elements and the gunas and the chakras (I did not really understand it then) and the mystical, yet organized and even logical, movement of energy dynamics.

In the early days of my work and study, I was intrigued and confused much of time.

"How can you sense someone else's energy with just your hands and your intention and attention and awareness? How could contacts on the body be so powerful and have such corrective effects? Why have I not heard about this type of work?" My questions were endless.

The answers were a long time coming, but those answers are perhaps the most important I will ever receive. They are now sacred questions and answers about my sacred contract with healing.

So I learned about the elements as descriptions of the substance and form of the human being and all creation. Earth, water, fire, air, ether, the five elemental principles of polarity therapy, became my model for redefining the challenges of my dis-eases and diagnoses. Somehow the idea of "imploded fire" became more palatable than the admonition I had heard for so many years, "Get over it. You're just mad."

It made sense to me that I was holding something unexplainable and profoundly internal. It made sense that the bodymind was capable of holding my life experiences as forces that created dis-ease in my body.

The principles of polarity therapy made sense when everything else was just medical chatter that made me angrier than I already was. It made sense that a trigger point was the experience of deeply earthing pain in my tissues such that it (pain) needed to be systematically unearthed to provide relief and restore function.

The polarity therapy tenets of balance and harmony in all matters of health and healing became my new commonsense ideas. These were laudable goals whether I was dealing with diet or exercise or supplements or bodywork sessions or even lifestyle issues and relationships. It just felt right to view my journey to wellness through such an enlightening and uplifting lens. The possibilities for a hopeful future were limitless in this new perceptual field called energy healing. I felt better about my experiences of medical conditions and symptoms gone wild. I applied the messages and methods of this new technology of health to every complaint.

I learned energy exercises and explored relationships between and among elemental proclivities and presence or lack thereof. I redefined my being-ness and learned from the holdings of my past on my present and future health and happiness.

This New Age healing system is called energy medicine. You've heard me mention it dozens of times so far in this book. I think this description only makes sense to those who study it. In some ways, this label is also its Achilles heel. Yet, when all is said and done, energy healing will be known, as it should be.

I have come to believe the truth of the saying about "all things in time." Pioneer that I am, I always realized the relative disadvantages of being a part of something new and revolutionary in the human experience. I kept studying and experimenting with the exercises and holistic concepts and moving forward anyway. My survival depended on it!

Today, I am humbled to be a part of such an awesome calling. As the years pass, I no longer fear the unknown or the will of unbelievers. I live as I believe and pray for discernment at every turn.

Polarity therapy and myotherapy were an amazing pair. I was about 16 months into the myotherapy sessions when I pursued polarity therapy training in 1995. The union of these two modalities was imbued with healing power of which I still stand in awe and wonder. On days when I just need to find the center of my being or to resource myself from within, polarity therapy serves as an anchor in the storm.

It would take pages to inform my readers about this work to a creditable degree so I will invite you to try it if it "feels right." The availability of the work has increased measurably since I started my studies.

I took a few advanced classes in polarity therapy as time and resources became available. Constant study and practice kept my learning curve afloat for a few more years until the next big thing came along. In 2010, I completed the two-year course of study for the R.P.P., registered polarity practitioner, status with Dr. Johnny Henderson and Tom Langan of Somatic Energy Therapies—now located in Berkeley Springs, WV.

In 2012, I became a board certified polarity practitioner (BCPP). Sometimes I have to pinch myself to believe all these accomplishments were granted to someone who was once so lost and broken. I am so deeply grateful.

The cranial wave comes in

Before I sought advanced studies in polarity therapy, the next "big thing" in my awakened healing process came from the same A.P.P. teacher, Roger Gilchrist. The cranial wave was knocking at my door and calling my name. My next dance with energy medicine school-work would be even longer and more intense. It started in 1997 with a pilot course that swiftly matured into a full-blown course in biody-namic craniosacral therapy in 1998.

Another faceless name appeared, unless, of course, you have an understanding of anatomy. "Cranio" was a close reference to cranium or skull, the enclosure of the brain and "sacral" was pretty clearly related to the sacrum, the wedge-shaped bone at the bottom of the spine. The words had very specific meanings but everything in between was missing.

A cranial hold was just simply a way of cradling someone's head. What did that have to do with pain relief? In my as-yet unenlight-ened mind, tides (a pivotal concept of energy movement) were oceanic phenomena, not human phenomena. If the tide was high, there was no beach to sit on. If the tide was low, one could sunbathe and swim in comfortable, fun-filled intervals.

Now I was being asked to not only grasp a new understanding of old ideas but also to palpate the experience in a human being on a treatment table. If the tide is at the head, it is called "inhalation." If the tide is moving toward the feet it is called "exhalation." This can't be true. These words describe breathing at its most basic level.

Primary respiration? Secondary respiration? What is the difference? What is the significance? The Health Within? These words had a familiar ring. As energy medicine terms, these concepts were unclear and intangible, at best. A persuasive perceptual shift was necessary for me to grasp the import of what I was learning about patterns of subtle energy movements.

Craniosacral therapy would give me more experiences of healing in my years as a student than I would ever have imagined possible. After my three-year course of study, my pain was in remission most of the time. Panic attacks were few and far between, and I was able to recover with remarkable speed from most episodes. Setbacks that had lasted for two to three weeks now only lasted for a week or three to five days. The intensity of my physical pain was so reduced that I was amazed at the results myself.

I could probably write a book about the sessions that created all the miracles. I don't know that it would mean as much to others as it does to me. I have already described a few of my most transformative experiences in the Born Angry Chapter.

Perhaps you can recall the "born again" story about the session with Mother Mary that integrated my birth experience. I came through the birth canal with light all around my being cleansing me of trauma. I saw the face of God! Clear and bright and forever blessed, I was reborn with more health and vitality and less pain. I *knew, saw and felt* the very presence of the Breath of Life.

When I arrived home that day, I noticed significant changes in my visual acuity and physical presence. I knew something was very different that was yet to be discovered.

It is a well-known phenomenon that healing effects have a mind of their own as it relates to time. There are the rare occasions when the effects are virtually instantaneous, but most take time to integrate. I think I experienced a little of both on that glorious day. I will share more of the details.

It was my turn to walk the dogs when I got home from class, so I got right to it. As I walked down the front stairs at 2030 Flagler Place, I was stumbling over my feet. In fact, I almost fell down the stairs except for my graceful dancer legs.

I was very joyful and a little overwhelmed by the events of the day. Full of bliss, I strolled with Foster through the neighborhood until I noticed that as I walked my balance was impaired. I was walking off the sidewalk and out of line for one so physically organized as I usually was. Foster must have been really confused.

By the time I rounded the block to my front door, I was in a glowing epiphany of healing. I can still feel the sensations of light around my eyes and in my being, an inner rejoicing. In those moments, I was aware of physical changes in my body. I would later recognize that I had experienced a remission of the pain in my limbs. It is my sense that a deep reorganization and integration of the fascia had occurred. The Breath of Life had restored the integrity of my tissues, at least, in part.

Soon I realized that there was something different about my eyes. My vision was better without my glasses. How could that be? I removed my contact leases as soon as I got in the door. Glasses were okay for dog walking, but my vision was usually a bit blurred right after removing my lenses. Once in a while, I fell asleep with my lenses in my eyes, but I knew this wasn't a good idea, so I was careful about it. There was no question: My eyesight was clearer, and I felt whole and strong.

I traveled through space and time to the essence of life itself in the arms of Mother Mary, my shamanic leader. The universal

Mother had channeled the Source into my bodymind to refresh and bless my wholeness. More importantly, a great life lesson was given, a messianic gift. I was healed, and so it is. Now, I must tell the world and teach those who will learn. Our beneficent creator had bestowed upon me another amazing *gift with responsibilities.*

The miracle of the pain remission was one of many significant outcomes of my bodywork sessions on the table. My walk through life was forever changed. Not only was I rehabilitated in my body, I was a believer for all time in the power of the Breath of Life, an important component of the work of biodynamic craniosacral therapy.

One day I may catalog my healing experiences so that I can get the full import—or not. Suffice it to say at this point that I am as yet so awed by them that quantification seems pointless. In many ways, any one of them carries the power of all of them.

I cannot close this section without answering the question, *What is craniosacral* therapy? Perhaps it appeared for a moment that I was just mesmerized by the Breath of Life and forgot to explain. I would never leave my readers hanging. So here goes.

Craniosacral therapy is derived from a specialty practice in osteopathic medicine, according to Roger Gilchrist in his book, *Craniosacral Therapy and the Energetic Body.* The "Cranial Concept" originated by Dr. William Garner Sutherland was inspired by his experiences as a medical student and by the work of osteopathy's founder, Dr. Andrew Taylor Still. Sutherland's cranial osteopathy concept established an approach to health care that emphasizes the intrinsic motion of the body.

Craniosacral therapy is a way of working with the core of human experience at all levels—physical, mental, emotional and spiritual. Craniosacral therapists are trained in the art of palpation and perceptual orientation as a way of contacting the inherent wisdom of Health in the body.

This explanation from Gilchrist's book is elucidating:

The biodynamic approach works with the energetic forces underlying symptoms, and helps those forces find their natural state of balance. This allows for a reorganization in the tissues and energy patterns of the body that come from within . . . the client's body is encouraged to find its own resolution to the conditions it has held.

Perhaps my most useful and profound learning from all of my studies in craniosacral biodynamics has to do with the stillness that is the groundswell of all motion. My experience of the dynamic stillness was life altering and had a dramatic effect on my view of physical and spiritual presence.

There is no duality at this level of being, according to Dr. Michael Kerns: "This is the realm from which all motion and expressions of life emerge."

I still have a hard time containing this idea without shouting, Wow!

The fundamental skills associated with therapeutic presence, such as negotiating space and holding neutral along with practitioner anchors like grounding and centering have become my way of life in 2014. Moreover, the quality of lovingness that undergirds the practice of craniosacral biodynamics and polarity therapy is my guiding light.

The sum total of my enlightenment as a student of energy medicine is expressed in my very first paper on the subject, *What Polarity Therapy Means to Me*. A requirement for application for A.P.P. status, the concluding paragraph says it best:

As I reflect on the principles and concepts of Polarity Therapy, I find one which endears me to the work in its

149

fullest. The first principle of Love or what I call, the quality of lovingness, which one must possess to do this work, is of itself transforming. Love is the core of the resonance that makes Polarity Therapy do its wonderful magic. It is the supreme energy that leads us to the Breath of Life and keeps us in the light of life. I cannot think of a more peaceful, joyous and humble way to live than sharing lovingness with the universe.

I wrote these words in 1997 just as I was beginning my studies in craniosacral therapy. This profound life lesson reflected my early sentiments about the measurable and observable effects of energy medicine treatments on my health and my life. This idea about lovingness was the catalyst for the central theme of this book: Love Is the Answer. Again I say, "Amazing Grace!"

The breath

Speaking of power, I just realized that I have omitted to share a miracle that quite literally took my breath away. Somewhere between my beginnings with myotherapy and energy medicine, I found my foremost power: my breath.

Interestingly enough, I initially found this power in a doctor's office and not on the treatment table. I was still in the pain clinic phase of my healing journey when this power came. However, it started out like everything else as a tortuous process that seemed to take forever.

The frustration and anxiety that came with learning to tense each muscle group and breathe continuously for 20 minutes was hell in motion. The endless homework assignment of scripting every panic attack and anxiety reaction for six weeks was recharging and painfully ungluing for most of those weeks. When I started biofeedback, I did not know how to write about my panic experiences without reliving them. At first, I was often retraumatized by the exercise. Six weeks later I was less panicky and less painful. Biofeedback worked!

Dr. Fitzgerald, the psychometrist who took me on this journey, was easy enough to work with. Truly, all else had failed. I don't know how and where I found the perseverance and fortitude to proceed though such a humiliating retraining, but persevere I did.

I am once again so grateful to our magnificent Creator who just kept giving me gifts that manifested miracles.

I am not even angry that it always took days and weeks and months for things to fully work. I appreciate the grind that I was somehow willing to undertake to save myself, by the grace of God. Dogged determination strengthened my case and my results. I also learned to acknowledge that it is almost impossible to undo with all due speed the grievous damage we do to ourselves for years with blatant disregard for the consequences.

So I learned to breathe consciously. However, it is perhaps one of the hardest things that I ever had to describe. Biofeedback training was the primary label for the technique that was being applied to measuring and monitoring stress responses to specified triggers.

I would verbalize a recent panic episode, detailing the "activating event" and what I felt. The doctor would coach me through the prescribed breathing technique to restore my calm while monitoring my responses with electrodes. The breathing exercise was then called progressive relaxation procedure. Today, it has many names and variations. I made some general references to this process earlier, but I think there is more to be gained with a little further exploration.

Dr. Fitzgerald gave me a handout describing the procedure and instructed me to practice twice a day until I became proficient at a 20-minute session. It took many 45-minute trials to arrive at an effective 20-minute routine. But I did arrive at that time-sculpted threshold after 12 weeks of diligent practice and coaching.

No one could have told me what a power I was choosing. For this reason, I understand why it is so hard to teach others about this power called the breath. I'll even call it The Breath. It is that important. In fact, this is the reason that I write this book.

I guess I trusted the process even when I didn't know that I trusted the process. I started out with lots of resistance in the tissues of my breathing apparatus. It was nearly impossible for me to take any deep breaths in the beginning or to try to engage continuous breathing for more that a minute or two. Like many people, my lungs were tight and tenacious in their acquired form of shallow breathing. At the time, I had no clue to the difference I was seeking, but I kept on trying anyway. I was bound and determined to stop killing myself and to start healing myself. Imani ultimately confirmed this need for self-actualization.

Twice a day, I found a comfortable seat and, starting with my feet, trained myself to isolate and tense and relax my painful muscles while breathing in an organized and quantifiable cadence. I counted the seconds in between each set of movements. From my feet to my teeth, I followed all my body parts in the sequences assigned by the regimen.

Weeks later, I was amazed at what practice could achieve. The fuzzy places in my body became clear and available. The calmness I was seeking came within my own control and that of structured breathing. The empowerment that this lifesaving procedure brought with it would support all my years of healing practices. Ironically, I now understand that the far-reaching effects of concentrated conscious breathing cannot be described in words. This miracle of miracles can only be experienced. I invite you to embrace your breath and what it can do for you.

As I continued my energy medicine studies and SynergyDance practices, I would learn to use conscious breathing in so many other ways. The foundation was provided for the myriad techniques, exercises and forms of breathing for healing purposes that each new discipline offered. I used many variations, from the "Ha breath" of polarity therapy (and yoga) to manage the fire to alternate nostril breathing for brain integration.

I incorporated breathwork in my healing baths, meditations and my general presence in the world. I can tune into chakras, settle into center and energize myself with this amazing, God-given gem. Breathing would be primary until I learned yet another profundity, that breath or respiration, as thought of in everyday life, is indeed, secondary. But I'm getting ahead of myself again! Stay with me.

Breathwork is now my go-to self-help technique. For the record though, it would be some years after I learned how to breathe consciously that I would know the true supremacy of what I had embodied. For the most part, in the beginning, I simply felt more in control of my responses to panic and anxiety. I noticed that my pain seemed to calm when my nerves calmed. There was a connection between them that my inherent Intelligence knew all too well.

I also understood more about the psychology of the mind under the influence of panic and extreme anxiety. I knew about triggers and activating events and all sorts of concepts that made sense of my altered experiences. I did not yet understand the workings of the autonomic nervous system, sympathetic, parasympathetic and all that stuff. But I knew that my panic reactions were legitimate, measurable, instinctive human responses to certain stimuli under given conditions.

At last, I was validated in ways that were a little less crazy to the casual observer. The groundbreaking revelations about breathwork were extremely useful for the direction in which I was going. Remember, this treatment process with Dr. Fitzgerald predated energy medicine and my study of anatomy and nervous systems.

I would eventually study the "fight or flight" response in the body. I would learn to palpate and balance the autonomic and central nervous systems. Energy medicine would inspire and instruct these understandings in great measure and add confidence to my experiences of self-healing. I finally had personal knowledge of my inner responses along with the capacity to alter their expressions in the direction of Health.

The Health Within

This is an undeniable concept whose time has come. From an intellectual point of view, these three words manifested one of my most stunning perceptual shifts during my studies in craniosacral therapy. I needed a positive side to my life when this idea came into my awareness. The Health Within, largely synonymous with the Breath of Life, is worth mentioning for its nuance and intangibleness.

The idea of Health with a capital "H" as an active principle in the body overtook my understanding of human nature.

It made so much sense that our loving Creator would have formed us with "Health"—as a self-correcting, inherent life force. Health is not something given from the outside but is a presence on the inside that has volume and intention and connection to the Source of all life. Better yet, it is something to which we have access, our inner physician.

I know that I experience the Health Within every time I heal a wound with or without a Band-Aid. I understand that in a couple of weeks there will probably only be a scar and not an open sore. Yet, in the past, I gave all the healing credit to the Band-Aid or medicine that I put on it. I did not know about the innate wisdom that is alive within the cells of my body.

Like most folks, I had learned to accept a scar as a necessary punishment for an injury, not realizing that, much of the time, healing does not require scars.

There is no wealth beyond knowledge of the innate power of the Health Within and all that it embodies. I carry this thought with me and honor these capital letters with enormous reverence and appreciation for the light it gives to my life. I offer this idea of the Health Within as food for thought to those who need to understand more than they can see.

Health with a capital "H" may be defined as the presence of the Breath of Life in the cerebrospinal fluid, "liquid light" in the words of Dr. William Sutherland. Maybe these words are an oversimplification for all its value and importance. Yet, at its best, Health is the presence of Source energy in our beings. And it is always there unless we are dead. Health is, however, always around us even when our capacity to receive it is diminished. Health is the eternal promise of God.

So how do we loose touch with this Health so that we take on dis-eases that destroy us? I can't tell you the answer to this question with as much conviction. Right now, for me, it depends upon what you believe about life in general.

For instance, I believe in sacred contracts and free will and that we are all created for distinct purposes and journeys and that Spirit knows all. I believe that individuals choose their soul's journey in concert with many factors and influences and interconnections the whole of which I am not meant to understand. I believe in Caroline Myss's archetypes, Wayne Dyers' inspired living, Deepak Chopra's spiritual laws and The Bible of Jesus, the Christ.

I believe that when the student is ready the teacher will come. I believe in the Health Within. I believe that we either choose to diminish Health Within or expand it for reasons that are often far from our knowing as in past lives and causes right before our very eyes like abuse.

I believe we must seek to know more about healing for everyone's sake. I believe I am a messenger of God's gifts with responsibilities. The Health Within is one of the most meaningful and masterful among them all.

The Breath of Life

Breath is secondary? Who says? I did not think that I got that one by you. But it was worth a try. And, yes, I said breath, as we know it, is, indeed, secondary.

Now that you are sitting down, perhaps you are ready for yet another amazing grace of my healing experiences. I would imagine by now that you are beginning to understand why I have emphasized healing grace as another important theme of this book. Only grace could explain these stories.

Once again I look to the discipline of craniosacral therapy for an idea that needs a little more explanation and whose time has come. A primary respiration under the breath of air is the place to know the Breath of Life. A palpable presence in the fluid fluctuations of the living system, primary respiration defines the movement of the Breath of Life. The Breath of Life is primary in that it must always be present in the organism for life to exist, even when respiratory breath, as we understand it, is not present.

This concept is tricky to write about, so I will not attempt an in-depth discussion. I offered a brief definition in Chapter Two.

What I can do best is share my most tangible experiences of knowing the presence of the Breath of Life. Most times, it has been a clinical experience in a therapeutic environment. In many, many of my craniosacral therapy classes, I had the distinct feeling of holding the Breath of Life. It was part of our training. In the words of a long ago commercial, "It is indescribably delicious." I would add, "It does miraculous things."

I have personally experienced many "healings" associated with the presence of the Breath of Life as an energetic phenomenon that can be sensed through proprioception. Most times, the results were swift and remarkable!

Let me say a little more about proprioception. This term

describes the science of palpation. According to Michael Kern in *Wisdom of the Body,* palpation can be defined as sensing with the hands.

Dr. Kern explains further, "This (palpation) is a process by which information is transmitted to the brain by sensory nerve endings in the fingers called proprioceptors. The fingers contain the highest amount of nerve proprioceptors of any area of the body, making them acutely sensitive to even the most minute of impulses."

When I first read these statements, I was amazed beyond measure once more by the human design.

Another energy medicine pioneer, Dr. Harold Magoun, states that, "The human hand has been called the greatest diagnostic instrument known to man."

In craniosacral work (and polarity), hands are used as "perceptual antennae." The fingers learn how to think, how to feel and how to see. These ideas capture the essence of the magic and mystery of energy medicine practices. I imagine that many traditional doctors would agree with Dr. Magoun.

So let's get back to my Breath of Life (BOL) stories. But at least now you know how energy therapists palpate or sense the BOL, a.k.a., the Health Within.

I have conducted sessions with clients and practitioners who have similar claims about the "presence" of the Breath of Life and associated relief that can be noticed and/or felt. I think, more important, I have "real life" examples that hold the same likeness to "the truth and nothing but the truth" about the BOL. I will cite a few examples.

Just to get something started in familiar realms, I will start with the idea of the Holy Spirit. For some of you, this may generate more questions for a moment, but I will get to the physical example next. Just hold on!

The Holy Spirit is a spiritual phenomenon that is considered to be "a felt experience" by most or, at least, many Christians. There are many practicing believers who hold fast to the idea and can cite their own examples of Holy Spirit healings. I liken the presence of the Breath of Life to the presence of the Holy Spirit. It is no surprise then that Dr. Sutherland selected this term for the highest energetic vibration from the Book of Genesis in the Holy Bible.

Like the presence of the Holy Spirit, the Breath of Life sometimes yields results that are simply amazing. It is almost always predictably unpredictable, uncontrollable and unlike any force known to the five senses. It is God made manifest!

One of my best stories about a Breath of Life healing in the physical body takes place right within my family. This may sound a bit biased, but I am courageous enough to tell it anyway. Trust me, if your neck is out of joint and holding your shoulder hostage, there is no question about when it returns to its rightful place. It stops screaming at you!

This is what happened in Orlando during one of my rare excursions with my daughter, Sylver. She was performing with CHIC for a week at Disney and I was along for the fun.

As circumstance would have it, one of my first assignments was not in the domain of fun. Or so I thought. Sylver was experiencing severe neck pain and associated misalignments. She was not a happy camper. And there was the little problem of twelve shows to perform.

But never fear, Mother, the energy worker is here. To make a long story short, we prepared a table on her bed and proceeded with a craniosacral/polarity treatment.

Within a very short time of palpating and resonating with the subtle energy patterns in Sylver's system, a clearly recognizable energetic force became present to the area around her neck. As I held her neck in my hands, we both felt a connection that was tangible. It was so strong that I was energetically pushed away as the movement passed through the tissues and vertebrae in Sylver's neck.

I recall saying to her that something powerful had just happened and that I had nothing to do with it. I *knew* that her neck would be better. This may be an oversimplification, but it was like being in the right place at the right time and, I guess, choosing the right thing.

Sylver was the true beneficiary of this Breath of Life experience. Both the pain and dislocation were relieved. And, of course, she could brag that her mother, with the healing hands, had been directly responsible. Only I knew that the Breath of Life was responsible.

To be fair to the universal consciousness, it is important for me to mention here that the day that this all happened was a "High Holy Day" in the energy medicine network. The planets were shifting and opening portals beyond the veil such that believers were holding special prayer vigils. It was a sacred, light-filled opportunity for those whose resonance allowed access to its power. I was fortunate to have a numerology expert or two in my bag of tricks who could help my journey.

Was it the Breath of Life at its best potential? Was it the Breath of Life just doing what it does? Was it just that my hands were in the right place at the right time to feel a spontaneous healing?

What is the Breath of Life? I will probably never really scratch the surface in all my attempts to describe it in words. I can say with conviction that I hope you have the opportunity to experience the BOL and that it changes your life for the better, as it did mine. Then I hope that you will pass on the good news about energy medicine!

Approximate normalcy

Speaking of the power of positive psychology, I was given another potent gift from my friend, mentor and healer, Dr. Reynolds: the concept of approximate normalcy. I had no idea at the time how important a role these words would play in my spiritual rehabilitation. I am not even certain that I really understood why or how I would pull this off. My inner knowing received it clearly though, and I set out to accomplish this end as best I could. I trusted Dr. Reynolds' advice.

I also trusted the epiphany that arose in my spirit as I sat and meditated at my best friend's house in Fort Lauderdale, Florida, many years later in 2006. Taking a bit of respite while reveling in the wonderful day I was having, I recalled fondly those two power words, *approximate normalcy,* and their healing power.

At best the words are clear, but then what is normalcy? How is "normalcy" measured so that I could "approximate" it?

It was my walk with the reality of my disabilities that made this idea worth its weight in gold. Cold-sensitivity required me to wear layers upon layers of clothing that could have made me look like a monster from out of space or a football player or just plain out-of-season year round. Rather than appear odd and odder still just because of my clothing, I gave much practice and experimentation to the art of dressing so that I could look "normal" and not like I was trying to stay warm.

Constant pain in my back and legs caused me to walk with a cane for several years. I carried the prettiest cane I could find (it looked like an umbrella to most observers), and I walked as normally as I could. I smiled through the pain so that I would not always appear to be suffering. I worked hard to maintain the appearance of a normal life in all the ways that I could muster.

I breathed inconspicuously in public places so as not to bring attention to my constant pursuit of self-therapy. I participated in the church choir and worked at productive activities to stay engaged in a so-called "normal" life. This meant that I had to work at something. The "somethings" came along just as I needed them. The universe supported this challenge and I kept it close to my heart. I have just started to share this idea publicly now that I can make some real sense of it to share.

As I sit here today reflecting on my visit to Florida, I am proud to wear this expression about normalcy as a symbol of God's love for me. I had a delightful time with Gloria and her wonderful husband, Tony, and a few of their special friends as well. It was Mother's Day, and I was basking in the beauty of sunny Florida.

We had brunch on the water with Nick and Nadia and Vitto and then strolled to the theatre for a rendering of Bizet's *Carmen,* my favorite opera. So, of course, I was in ecstasy.

Yet as I lay down to nap and wait for Gloria and Tony to come home for the evening, I mused about how those words—approximate normalcy—enabled me to get the very best out of that fun-filled day.

I had prepared my layers with precision and perfection. My long pink skirt with the handkerchief hem was perfect for wearing matching pink capri leggings underneath so no one could notice (over toeless silk stockings). My pink satin jacket, the height of fashion in spring 2006, camouflaged the long-sleeve bodysuit undergarment and heat pack shoulder pads that were added in the ladies room at the theatre just before curtain time.

I wore the most comfortable, ankle-strap, multicolored (shades of pinks, etc.) high-heel open-toe shoes, so I could walk with a little sass like most preening peacocks on a high holy day. Mother's Day is kind of like Easter for women. I walked like I was taught as a debutante, carried an imported scarf and sported my newest Sylverwear jewelry.

My white leather coat was stored in the car for extreme temperature challenges. Nothing could go wrong! And nothing did! The theatre was pleasant and not cold at all so there was no reason for alarm or the coat. I looked as normal as any other mother, whatever that is.

The bottom line was that I did not look "disabled" or even challenged for that matter. From all appearances I was not in pain, not afraid, not cold, not crazy, not suffering and not different in ways that made people consider me less than okay.

Illness was considered a sign of weakness, bad luck and punishment by God during the era in which I grew up. In many ways, it still is. Since I knew that I wasn't weak, the victim of bad luck or being punished by God, I understood the importance of appearing strong, fortunate and loved by God.

Dr. Reynolds had decreed the doctrine of Approximate Normalcy and I followed it.

When I started to write these words, I connected deeply with this priceless lesson. The bliss and joy was immeasurable, and I knew this therapeutic idea to be among the things that worked!

I would have a similar experience of joy and bliss a month or so later at a going-away surprise party for a member of my niece's C.P.A. firm. Her party was a sad day for us, but we joined the group at the bowling alley with supportive hearts. It was my first time in a bowling alley in about ten years. I was certain that I would not participate in the game and that would be okay.

The universal mother had another plan. I was well layered that day so I started in a good comfort zone. The AC was moderate, and I was wearing a very cute hat. I was admittedly a little nervous about explaining why I was not going to bowl. It was a favorite family sport.

Yet as the opportunity grew closer, I realized that I was once again going to take a risk and exhibit approximate normalcy. I was going to bowl as if I were not at all disabled. So I found a ten-pound ball, which turned out to be too light, and turned in my name. I *would* do this, but carefully and intelligently, I told myself.

Now perhaps the true significance is not ringing out here. What is so hard about making a decision to bowl? It was about that same time that I was stricken by yet another injury to my right arm and elbow. I was in more pain that I had recently become accustomed to. I was worried about aggravating the pain and disability that I was already suffering.

Granted this was not a new dilemma, but the relapse was very fresh in my mind. It was difficult not to be restrictive and protective after all. Bowling wasn't mandatory, but that day, it was indeed just that. I needed to be normal or approximate normal on that very day. It was a risk worth taking for my soul's journey. It did not matter that I had the physical strength of a gnat most of the time. It did not matter that I had even less strength when injured. I was compelled to get in the game!

And get in the game I did. I played a full ten frames and even got a strike and a couple of spares. My coordination was awkward, my control was limited and it felt really funny in the moment. Yet, getting in the game was empowering to my aggrieved spirit. I needed to appear normal in spite of the pain and eventual aggravation.

There was no question as to whether or not there would be further injury. It was impossible to avoid it under such circumstances. But the more I suffered pain and disability, the more I understood the need to fight against it and resist its overpowering control over my life.

The tendency to always be defeated by less than perfect abilities or handicaps (the inability to wash my hair or carry groceries) sometimes simply *must* be overcome, God willing. This is one of the lessons that approximate normalcy taught me.

So I bowled one game and cheered and high-fived everybody (another painful activity for me) and ate and celebrated a dear friend's new life. I was blissful and joyful for having done it, but I was also sore afterward and required some recovery time. I will long remember the joy. The pain will come and go.

There are those who would argue the obvious imperfections of such a philosophy of life. Perhaps I pick the wrong day and do real, irreversible harm. Perhaps I am just faking, which lacks integrity. Or perhaps I am embracing remembered wellness, an idea whose time has come. Perhaps will always be a valuable consideration and right or wrong will rarely be apparent. Choice is freedom. That is the lesson. Positive choice empowers. That is the miracle.

Work Therapy

Some things make sense because they just make sense. This is true of work therapy. If, indeed, you are someone who has been productive and prolific, as I was before disaster struck, becoming uninvolved in life will lead to even more dis-ease and disorder regardless of the cause.

The condition of permanent disability leads decidedly in this direction. It is almost impossible to move forward and heal when life requires nothing from you. Full-time therapy alone, unless inclusive of work-related therapies, is insufficient to the journey of the human soul. The possible exception is in the cases where individuals come to teach medical lessons. I think you get my meaning.

Some surprising opportunities came into my life that fulfilled this necessity for work therapy, which I defined as something that produced results that mattered. I had to approximate normalcy, as Dr. Reynolds had taught me.

It had become impossible for me to hold a job on a daily basis, and I was no longer working for the government. I was suffering a great deal and unable to do much that made any real sense. Then providence brought the first glimmer of hope.

It came to me through my sister-in-Christ, Bernice Ross. She asked me to teach her grandchildren piano lessons.

This request was a big laugh to me when she first broached the subject. I could not believe what I was hearing. I had never taught piano lessons, although I had maintained my ability to read music all my life and never lived anywhere without a piano.

But these were not qualifications for teaching piano lessons. And while I did have piano as my minor in college and legally enough credits in music to qualify as having a music minor, giving lessons was not something to which I had ever given any consideration. Frankly, Bernice did not care about the formal qualifications. She thought I would make a good teacher for her grandchildren. That is what mattered to Bernice. I was honored.

We were choir buddies. Bernice was a committed Christian and all those she helped were always changed for the better. I was a willing beneficiary. Somehow I knew (there is that *knowing* again) that Bernice was asking me to do something God would want me to do. I could not refuse her request or her insistence on paying for my services.

I purchased a few beginner books, refreshed my recollection of their familiar pages, practiced my lessons and proceeded to follow the call. These actions gave me purpose and pleasure. For those special half hours each week, I was normal and whole and worthwhile. I was contributing and making a difference in the lives of children. What a remarkable blessing! Each of them was a little healer on my long journey. Teaching piano was my first work therapy as a disabled person. I loved it!

Who knew the weekly piano lessons I hated as a child and the hours of error-filled practice would lead to nirvana? I was a good teacher. The students learned scales and songs and gave recitals at my home. Bernice became my third student. Her grandson and then my brother's daughters, Michele and Danielle, were next. Melanie, a younger sibling, also sang in our last recital.

This music-centered work therapy was truly my saving grace! I would get two more students, the daughters of a family friend, and many offers in the seven years that I taught beginner piano lessons.

I was not that proficient as a pianist and never played for anyone other than in my home for myself. But God and Bernice expanded my horizons way beyond my own view of myself. Teaching piano lessons was a healing experience of great value and life-lasting memories.

After all teaching was in the genes. I had a M.Ed. and the desire for wholeness that was willing to take the risk. I was an educational specialist for most of my early career. My great-grandfather founded an elementary school in Concord, NC. My father was a college president and my mother a college professor.

I loved to work with children. I learned this about myself while teaching dance to the campus kids at Voorhees. In many ways, I was uniquely qualified. Earth angel Bernice saw the potential and trusted God to fulfill the promise.

From time to time, I come across the piano books, recital programs and certificates that remind me of my music teacher days. It was a memorable part of my healing journey, but I only taught for a season of seasons. Nonetheless, this work therapy experience was the beginning of my return to productive normalcy and meaningful existence. This healing transition was another part of the puzzle that led me to spiritual growth and enlightenment.

The pursuit of training for myself and especially children was work that not only mattered but also that healed.

Yet another part of the puzzle was to set up a treatment room in my home so I could practice and experiment. My mother gave me the treatment table and the piano I used to teach my little healers, adding another dimension to the gift of healing. I studied and practiced faithfully.

I was journeying to a higher place in my being. The dawning of the healing potential of work therapy opened the door to even more opportunities to fulfill my sacred contract. Writing this book is my latest example of an endlessly shining therapeutic idea!

Sylverwear is born

The next big step would be longer lasting and equally awe-inspiring. It began in relationship to my childhood summers in church camps, participating in sports and games and crafts and just being a kid. Camp Baskerville on Pawley's Island, SC, was one of my favorites.

I remember sitting for hours making leather bracelets and beaded baubles to bring home to Mommy and Daddy to document our summer fun. My sisters, Leila and Camille, and my brother, John Jr., and I went to this camp together. We swam and stayed in the barracks and ran from mosquitoes and got toppled by the waves in the ocean. We told scary stories and I pretended to sleepwalk to entertain the girls in my cabin. It was a fun time and creative hands were in great demand. Who knew these creative hands would become a life raft to a failed spirit?

God knew. And that is all that was required for destiny to unfold. For unto us a child was born, a gift was given. It was called Jewel Chimes. This was the first name given to our line of jewelry when we decided to call it a business, although it was still a hobby.

The inclination for jewelry making grew out of my mother's commitment to engaging all her children in productive hobbies. In addition to church camps in the summers at the beach, we participated in youth conferences on the campus where we lived. Wherever we went, there were always crafts to keep us busy and out of trouble.

When I visited my sister, Camille, in the spring of 1995 in Charleston, SC, at Spoleto Festival time, as I did every year, I had no idea there would be a life-altering adventure in the making.

Camille had learned to make jewelry from Friendly Plastic™, a new material that had just been invented and was easily available. She had taken a class, a very Potts-like thing to do.

Camille taught me how to use the material. I taught Sylver as soon as I got home after my vacation. Handcrafted jewelry became the new family business for Sylver and me.

Foremost among the curiosities of our jewelry designing adventure was the precision touch that would emerge as Sylver created more and more designs that attracted the attention of onlookers. Rings, cuff links and hoop earrings rolled off her hands like identical twins molded by God's holy order. She had an unusual gift for balance and proportion that called forth opportunities for full exploration and expansion.

I, on the other hand, had occasional accuracy and a knack for abstraction that was also attractive to our small captive audience. Between the two of us, many creations were possible and the potential for great things was elusive and obvious at the same time.

We experimented with button covers and shoe clips and earrings in all shapes, sizes and colors. We wrapped stones and gems and invented unique alternatives to the current costume jewelry market. It did not take very long to find our niche in the fashion world.

With Sylver's stage wardrobe and signature style leading the charge, numerous design ideas were born. Her growing celebrity status as lead singer of CHIC charmed clients. Women and a few men understood what we were saying with our one-of-a-kind product that highlighted each individual's unique personality. Sylver schlepped our jewels around town and ultimately on international tours with CHIC in high profile venues.

Ten years later, Sylverwear had bragging rights for a website, online store and celebrity clients the world over. Television soap opera, *One Life to Live,* Yolanda Adams, Sir Elton John, Omar Hakim, Nile Rodgers, CHIC and The Montreux Jazz Festival soon joined the list of clients we boast about and wonder how we got so lucky.

Yet in the beginning, it was just a hobby. It was something that I could do no matter what condition I happened to be in. No matter how painful or panicky I was feeling, my newfound hobby was just the thing to stir my creativity and challenge my physical endurance and tolerances.

It was very hard at first to sit in a chair for long periods of time or even hold up my arms long enough to complete a set of earrings or a single centerpiece. (It is still hard!) I messed up a lot of plastic and made many monstrosities that made me laugh out loud. I made a lot of beautiful things as well and surprised myself often.

How could painful hands be so creative? How could all this come from an overmedicated woman who could barely get out of bed? God's healing grace was the only answer. Jewelry making was sufficient to keep me going through all the challenges that would come as we formalized a business out of our love for creativity.

My need for work therapy had found its own way through Sylverwear. I would never again be idle and worthless. My creativity would be my work therapy as long as my hands held the promises of God. And so it is.

In 2014, Sylverwear is poised to expand marketing and distribution of its celebrity brand with a new limited edition collection and a new slogan: "Feel Like A STAR! The Magic of Sylverwear. R U Rockin' Sylverwear?" Log onto: www.sylverwear.com!

Water therapy

I would be remiss if I did not mention my relationship with the water element in my healing process. Sometimes the obvious is not so obvious. In the case of water, it is my considered opinion that we take for granted this most available resource.

Again, quite coincidentally, I learned the power of water for many healing purposes. Once again, it started in the shower in the '70s when I was treating a sore back.

One of my prescriptions was to stand in the shower four times a day just letting the hot water run on my neck and back for 8 minutes. I often crawled down the hall to pull off this feat. Yet, in time, hot water therapy would yield positive results and aid my rehabilitation. This experience was a useful addition to my cellular memory in years to come.

I don't recall right now the exact winter that healing baths became my best friend. But I can still visualize sitting in the tub at 2030 Flagler Place thanking God for hot water and lavender bath salts.

The winters felt very, very cold in my early years of pain and suffering. I could not get out of bed most mornings because there was nowhere for me to go that was warm enough. Under the covers was as good as it got!

The healing power of water therapy became more clear early in my study of polarity therapy. I was struggling with learning about the elements but intrigued by all the possibilities. I had been instructed to use healing baths post-session to integrate the treatment effects. I was struggling with all the toxicity in my body, mind and spirit. I needed space within myself to reorganize and reorder my life force. I learned about the ether element and the need for internal spaciousness for optimum functioning and Health.

I trusted the tenets of polarity therapy and spent every morning in the tub, holding just one intention: space. It was another healing call that would be life changing. I lovingly embraced this new resource as it embraced me with daily comfort and relief. I found a new oasis of healing potential that would grow and expand in leaps and bounds over months of committed practice. Water therapy worked!

In time, the winter months became more bearable, and I had an organizing force to jump-start every day. These baths helped me to get through my studies in craniosacral therapy as well.

It was my regular practice to take baths after each class day. The baths made a significant difference in my ability to get through weeks of daily therapy and study. I came to *know* that the water element integrates healing and supports the treatment process.

170

Once again, something over which I had control came to my rescue. This was something I could do to help myself. There were times when I needed help keeping the tub clean. But I had help when I needed it. So this challenge was not a deterrent to my success. Family and friends did the honors when the need was great or just as a loving gesture. Water therapy is a gift that can make everybody feel better on any given day!

Water is my friend. I had learned this as a swimmer and I had taken water aerobics in one of the pain clinics. The Creator's wisdom championed my cause again. I will always practice various forms of water therapy—especially when I am blessed by a beautiful beach day.

Exercise, exercise, exercise

If I have an annoying bandwagon that drives my friends and family nutty, it is my love of exercise: Exercise or die! Exercise or die! Exercise or die!

I believe this in my heart of hearts. I learned this mantra in my healing process.

I would not be writing any of this if I didn't have organized, differentiated, persistent exercise in many forms. I exercised for years to retrain muscles and realign structures and strengthen tissues and retard atrophy and eradicate disability. And while the latter goal was not fully met, I did regain function and increased strength potential over time—with continuous exercise. I pretty much did eradicate the appearance of pain and disability as my literal walk through life became easier. Approximate normalcy helped!

I learned the dynamics of how the hipbones reflect the shoulder bones and even the anklebones. I recognized the importance of space in the joints as representative of spaciousness in life. I experienced decompression as healing my time in space, again and again.

I studied decompression as it relates to depression. I liberated my physical experience every time I held an A/O (atlanto-occcipital) joint release or executed a back-bending stretch exercise on the ball in my bedroom.

For most of my early years in therapy, my bedroom was as far as I needed to go to make sure my exercises got done. When I was discouraged and doubtful about my efforts, I could see the vision across the room. I could see myself in motion if I could just take those few steps from point A to point B to my exercise bike. If I could move to the edge of the bed, I could do my seated leg lifts, painful or not. I could execute directional, intentional, healing action on my own behalf. This was the greatest miracle of all. The adage, "Try, try, again," is truly sage advice.

Exercise is that kind of challenge for me. I try again and again, sort of like praying without ceasing. Growth and development are slow, but perfect when movements are executed properly. Finding the right activities for my body type and personality was key to the process. Frequency was more important that intensity. Changing exercise routines and regimens for ultimate flexibility was another part of the drill.

I've briefly mentioned my list of exercise training: I danced and swam and stretched everything I owned, used an exercise bike, had lots of physical therapy, did breathwork and on and on. The most important words here are "on and on."

At my best, I stretched every two hours and followed workout routines with hand weights twice a day for 45 minutes to an hour and a half. When I included a dance routine, my workout sessions could last for as long as two to three hours. I had preselected musical tapes that supported my chosen movement dynamics.

My student-centered nature had given me the discipline to practice, practice, practice. A lot of credit goes to my musical and theatrical pursuits for this empowering behavior and my strict upbringing. And, of course, six months in a pain clinic will give you little time for much else.

I am not certain, but I suspect exercise physiology myth-busting served me well here. The myth: The other guy or girl is doing it right. A related myth is that what the other person is doing is good for me. Third in the lineup of poor exercise psychology is the idea that I could teach myself all I needed to know about exercise.

The possible exception is walking for exercise. Pretty much we all know how to walk. Yet there are many exceptions when evaluating a walk routine for therapeutic purposes. As a culture, we also walk poorly and have challenged posture. So first, there may be a need for postural considerations in an exercise program. Did you know that an injury to the hips most surely means an injury to the shoulders? The alignment of structure is connected; no bone is an island.

There are a zillion examples of ways to exercise. For me, exercise was the difference between life and death. Amen. I truly believe that the Creator gave us the *Breath of Life* as the inertia for our ultimate motion and movement through life. God intended for us to care for ourselves and so endowed us with this internal physician. We must, however, know how to access the love within that heals and allow it to do its magic. Such action and trust on our parts can change the world.

Before I lose the meditators and stillness gurus, of which I am one, let me acknowledge that the greatest exercise of all, in my humble opinion, is the experience of oneness with God. This holiest of holies can heal all things. It is the ultimate exercise in life. Dynamic stillness, another craniosacral therapy concept, embraces this place of Health in a way that requires no observable motion, yet we know atoms are spinning and molecules are pulsing. To wit, there is motion in stillness.

Deepak Chopra discusses the idea of "effortless effort" in the mystical interpretation of the question of work and intention. The *Breath of Life* is effortless; it is not seeking Source. It is Source.

Polarity therapy contacts on the body generate synergistic responses in triads and triunes. If I touch your toes, I can heal your neck. If I hold your sacrum and occiput, I can calm your autonomic nervous system. If I practice squatting, I can prevent panic attacks and exercise my intestines.

So, yes, exercise can be stillness or meditation, contacts on the body or swimming laps. It is a very personal choice and should be evaluated in a way that guarantees success not just possibilities. It is a lifestyle choice that should give noticeable results that you cannot live without. Individuals who are in touch with the Healthy self can have this type of awareness to guide them. It takes attention, intention and action.

Regular exercise has been proven effective in the treatment of most dis-eases you can name, including depression and heart disease. I would add fibromyalgia. Exercise can also be fun and a good social outlet. I believe that it is important to execute exercise routines as precisely as possible. I also know that it is equally important not to take anything in life too seriously.

Returning to the myths that I posited a page ago, most folks think exercise has almost no rules. In some ways that is true. In many ways, that is another myth.

It is a widely known fact that most or at least many Americans either overexercise or get no exercise at all. The two most important rules are to not do either. Too much or none is just not good.

My next myth about exercise and the following one simply suggest that it is a good idea to do research and seek advice and counsel about the best workout for your body type and body challenges. The other guy at the gym (not the teacher) may be doing it right for him and may not be doing the right thing for you. Or he may be just the guy to help you learn, in which case you have a bonus: an exercise buddy. Support can be really good. Nothing is more powerful than a helping hand. Learn all that you can about your body physiology and alignment and all the stuff your awareness can grasp. You will live a more Healthful life.

There are myriad practitioners from trainers to myotherapists to massage therapists to chiropractors who understand the function and technology of exercise. Yoga and tai chi instructors and body psychotherapists and even polarity and craniosacral therapists are available all over the world. There are gyms and spas and retreats and all kinds of venues willing to train you to understand and effectively execute a well-tailored exercise regimen.

For people with limited access to practitioners, there are books and tapes and CDs and DVDs and cable TV. There are even people who will come into your home. Anything is possible if you believe, trust and seek it with all your heart. Be sure to set achievable goals and give your exercise routine your all, at least, until you get used to it!

Bottom Line: Exercise! Exercise! Exercise! Whether in stillness or motion, honor your being and your body.

CHAPTER 10

What Worked, Part 3: Gifts With Responsibilities

M Y ARC OF HEALING EXPANDED EXPONENTIALLY when I birthed the idea of gifts with responsibilities, my latest catch phrase for the healing love that dwells within each of us. A valuable retrospective on my sacred contract with healing, this idea is now the fulcrum of my beliefs about what works. I had to live through this life principle to know it personally and to espouse its significance. The realization that I could use what I thought of as my "everyday talents and abilities" to heal myself was a monumental awakening.

To understand that I am, indeed, "responsible" to use my "gifts" to the Glory of God took my breath away. I knew for certain: Love is the answer—God's and mine, together.

You have already read many stories about my dancer legs. So you already have a clue about the things I include on my list of gifts that heal. Running a real close second or maybe even side by side is my other great love, singing. Here's the whole story.

Singing for the Lord!

Sing! Sing! Sing! Whatever you do children, sing! I should write the song. It is Gospel, I believe. All God's children should sing! My philosophy is sing until something changes. Much like prayer, as far as I am concerned, singing is a form of prayer.

Singing has been my soul's delight since I was a little girl. I *knew* this gift was the jewel of my soul when I sang my first solo in the fourth grade. It was the first time I heard my singular voice outside of a group in an actual performance. It was an exhilarating experience! Thereafter, this solo was an annual event at my school at Christmastime.

I believe the lyrics to the song, *One Little Candle,* shaped my vocal attitude and my love for singing. The choir always sang this song last and I always closed the show.

I feel it is fortuitous that I started out with something loving to sing about as my defining moments. The closing line (my solo) became my soul serenade:

And if everyone lit just one little candle
What a bright world this would be.

Although I would have many ups and downs as a singer, especially when I was focused on a singing career, I would never really stop singing. Singing would have more therapeutic value in the whole of my life than almost any other thing I ever did. Dancing, sex and energy medicine would come close. Singing would always be my bedrock.

In recent years, I've named this gift, "Singing for the Lord." I was a choir member and soloist in the Episcopal Church for most of my early life. My mother was the church organist at the college where I grew up. So I was a natural. She was my accompanist; we were a duo. I cannot say that I felt very spiritual about singing then. I really did not like church that much. I was okay with reciting Bible verses. A little Sunday school was all right, though I don't think I really got it.

Religious practices felt much like the discipline I got at home so, at least, they were familiar. All the "thou shalt not's" sounded right somehow. I don't think I really knew who Jesus was then. My parents never really talked about Him. For the most part, church stuff, besides grace at meals and bedtime "Now I lay me's" was left at church. There was almost no religious dogma in my household. You just had to go to church and Sunday school without question. Refusal to participate was not an option.

I was taught to believe in God as I was taught everything else—intellectually. The mushy stuff would come later as I unfolded spiritually. In many ways, I am grateful for this outcome. Even though it was pretty quiet in my church, unlike the Baptists and other more upbeat denominations, I was at home in the peaceful environment. At least nobody openly hurt me there. I felt safe. I grew up without a lot of dogma and no real drama to turn me against organized religion.

Best of all, I loved to sing in the choir. I liked church music, especially Negro spirituals. My voice was particularly well suited to spirituals and to hymns and canticles for that matter. My classical training was a bonus.

Actually, my mother was my first voice teacher. My mother had an undergraduate degree in music from Virginia State College (with distinction) and a master's degree from the University of Michigan. She was an accomplished pianist and choral director.

When I started singing at the age of eight, a voice teacher of note visited my mother in our home in Denmark. At my mother's insistence, I auditioned for her and was told that I would grow up to be a mezzo-soprano. Of course, I was mostly a lyric in those days, but the insightful maestro could see what was to come. It was a defining moment in my life and I did grow up to be a mezzo as she predicted. This was a magnificent calling for a young girl who just started singing.

I trained with my mother for many years after that prophetic day. In spite of the vicissitudes of my "Daddy's girl" persona, my relationship with my mother was blessed by a harmonious musical connection. When she played and I sang, we were one, a loving pair. The bond was nurturing and whole. She was the pianist, and I was the singer. The combination was magical. This gift was one of the best parts of my early life.

Even when we disagreed about an interpretation or a song selection or vocalization, we had no real conflict. We made choices and lived with them and grew through them. I was impressed with her and she was impressed with me. There was no competition.

She knew how to pick songs that expressed the nuances of my vocal artistry. That was more than most of my other voice teachers could accomplish. Mother had a magnificent ear for a great song. She understood the colors and timbre of art songs and arias and folk songs and all sorts of classical and traditional genres. Her interpretations were impeccable and her piano touch was exceptionally moving and accurate.

Even when we weren't singing and playing together, I sat and listened to her perform family favorites with awe and respect whenever she favored us with her talents. It was a memorable family pastime. There was no greater joy in our home that the celestial sounds of *Somewhere Over the Rainbow, Liebestraum, Moonlight Sonata* or *Blue Butterflies,* the latter her signature melody. On rare occasions, our father played the violin. The entire family often sang and played in the parlor. Our family concerts were a treasure we all cherished.

So I sang in church and in the school choir in elementary school and high school and college and so on and so on. I competed in drama festivals and talent shows and traveled around with my signature aria, the *Habanera* from Bizet's *Carmen,* with my mom at the piano. I missed a high school prom because I was competing in an Omega Talent Show in Detroit, Michigan. I won third place, rare for a singer. My father, the Grand Basileus, was proud and, of course, my mother was ecstatic.

I also won first place in all the plays in which I participated during my high school years. A qualified thespian, I was surely headed for the stage. Life was good as long as I was singing, dancing and acting. Everyone seemed to agree that I would go off to college and become a star or, at least, an accomplished professional. If you asked the people I grew up around in my childhood what Paula Potts is doing, they would all ask without hesitation, "Is she still singing?"

There was a time I would resent that question, but that resistance did not last.

Blues get off my shoulders

There was also a time I sang the blues to soothe my inner turmoil. Whenever I was sad as a young teen and needed to vent or have a good cry, I would stand in the hall of mirrors in one of our presidential living rooms and sing a popular ballad, *Blues Get off My Shoulders*. Over and over I wailed and cry-ooned the languidly pulsing lyrics until I got whatever the weight was off my shoulders.

Usually, the tears were related to a break up with one of my boyfriends due to sexual difficulties. (I remained a virgin in high school.) Or the sad songs were a result of a fight with my mother for having that boyfriend in the first place. All girls with boyfriends were "bad girls" in those days unless, of course, the mother chose the boy.

My mother never liked most of my friends. She considered few of them qualified to mix with the daughter of the president. Friendship was a high-risk venture at best, worthy of extreme limitations. American bluebloods shunned the potential to encounter influences outside their class. Small towns did not have much else.

Urban music really began to touch my soul and heal my sins and sorrows during my adolescence. In my elementary school years, rock and roll music was mostly an excuse to shine on the dance floor.

You already know that I had lots and lots of problems as a youngster. Every adolescent nightmare was on my list that challenged my standing with my peers:

- Celebrity parents
- First Family in the Big House
- Good genes
- Light skinned
- Good clothes
- Great voice
- Great dancer
- Lead in all the school plays
- The best grades in school

Surely, no one had that many pluses on her card! So my school-mates decided the teachers must be giving me those grades because I was, after all, "the president's daughter, you know."

As fate would have it, both the elementary school and the high school that I attended had the same name as the college where my father was president. So many of my classmates thought he was the head of our school as well. There was no convincing them that my dad had no influence in school affairs.

In 2006, I wrote a poem called *President's Daughter*, which captures the heart of the matter. The opening verse reveals the impact of such a life on a young girl with so many advantages that turned out to be disadvantages:

President's daughter,
Game for the slaughter.
Who does she think she is?
She's not in show biz.
First child in the big house
On the hill
The pressure of privilege
Very little free will

So I guess I used my singing gift as a healing tool to conquer the blues long before I understood its potency as my divinely ordered responsibility. That's how good God is!

Retrospectively, I grew to recognize that my mother appreciated her gifts—five royal children to raise—and her responsibilities as role model, mentor and First Lady. She may have been far too strict with her protective instincts in my eyes then, but I now know she knew exactly what she was doing and the gifts she was giving us.

The *President's Daughter* poem concludes with sentiments that express my appreciation for the blessings of a gifted lifestyle so richly nurtured by my parents:

President's daughter
Grateful indeed
For the special title
She did not need.
Or so she thought
When yet a child
Now a great legacy
Her family's pride.

So let's return to the singing stories. Perhaps my most joyful experiences as a vocal student and performer came during the three summers I spent in music institutes at Virginia State College in the mid-'60s. My grandfather, who lived in the town of Petersburg, was often sitting in the audience at our concerts. I loved his support!

It was heaven on earth for me to live in a college dormitory and have the freedom to be on my own as a high school student away from home on a college campus, but nothing in my experience at that time in my life compared to singing and dancing and acting all day long for weeks on end.

I studied voice and piano and music theory and history. I performed the lead role of Anna, in *The King and I* and the oldest daughter, Liesl, in *Sound of Music*. I was perfect for the signature tune, *Sixteen Going on Seventeen* and the waltz—or was it the polka—in *Shall We Dance.* I sang solos and choral arrangements and attended concerts in amphitheaters in Philadelphia and New York. Those were glorious summers!

My return to the same college as a freshman music major would be fraught with ill health and overwhelming disappointments. I did not adjust well to college life. I spent way too many days in the infirmary with anemia and other symptoms. Once again, I seemed to attract all the bullies and bad boyfriends and eat all the wrong foods.

My nervous system and my digestion could not hold up under the pressure. I was sent home in January of the second semester with a diagnosis of total nervous exhaustion and 25 pounds lighter. (Fortunately, I had gained 10 pounds the summer before my sojourn to college.) I was 17 years old and totally confused by all that happened in those horrific five months of my first year in college.

I was too frail to continue with any major life activities. I was medically ordered to rest. I returned home to the college campus where I was raised—defeated and dejected. We all hoped that I would resume my college studies in the fall of that year.

But my humiliating departure from "freshman-hood" was not the worst part of the story. My life as a vocal music major was over. I had added insult to injury by trashing my voice along with my college career.

As a rather highly rated vocalist in the music department that first semester, I managed to get assigned to all the primary music groups and ensemble casts, from Rigoletto to *Ahmal and the Night Visitors* and the Christmas Concert and Sunday choirs. In addition to vocal technique lessons and piano lessons, I was cast in every production of note—not to mention all the other curriculum courses.

Thinking myself a real superstar, I would learn that over-singing really only made me super stupid, especially when I was sick. I kept a cold or virus most of the first semester. By the time I left college, I could not sing anything without cracking and embarrassing myself. For the next two years, I never sang a note in public for any reason.

It would be many years before I would sing again with confidence. My home has always been graced with a piano and I sang for myself whenever I needed to, which was often.

During those mute years, I sang only for myself at the piano in my living room when no one, not even my daughter, was around. Singing for myself to heal my soul became my private resting place.

It was a blessing that I had maintained my ability to read music. This made it easier for me to keep singing. I chose all my living arrangements with a primary consideration for the best home for my piano. Whenever Sylver and I moved, I always called the piano movers first. We moved quite a lot.

Whether spawned by tears or blues or even some good news, singing has always been a monumental blessing. I would sing again and understand it to be a unique part of my healing process. Singing worked!

When I became disabled from my unfortunate experiences at the pain clinic, I was a member of the choir at St. George's Episcopal Church, which I had joined four years earlier. Over the years, I had learned to love it there and enjoyed the opportunities to use my voice in public once again.

At that time, I was not working at all, including work therapy. I could barely get out of bed and walked with a cane. I was still on strong meds and recovering from the panic attack that sent me running out of the pain clinic. But when I had a moment's peace, I could sit at my piano and practice my choir music and feel whole and needed and appreciated and productive. My voice connected me to God and to my inner spirit that needed the comfort of the words I was singing.

I was free again. Singing is my true freedom, I have learned. When I could no longer drive myself to rehearsals, an angel came and made a way out of no way. Her name is Bernice Ross. She is my sister-in-Christ, and she carried my cross. She picked me up every Thursday for rehearsal and on Sunday mornings as well. She also brought me dinner on Sundays that I was too weak to cook after singing all morning. She is one of my favorite people in the whole world. She is a sister, a mother, a friend. I don't know how I would have been resurrected without her prayers and faithful assistance for so many years.

Bernice would accept no compensation for her consistent loving care. Even when I became better and taught her and her grandchildren piano lessons, she insisted on paying and would not let me barter for her services as a caregiver. She was my rock of strength in a weary land! Because Bernice was willing to be the gas in my car and see me to my next destination, I was able to grow stronger and stronger and ultimately take the reins again myself.

I prospered as a singer at St. George's and went on to start a gospel choir there with my cousin Rose and Bernice and other members. The "Voices of Praise" would expand not only my musical repertoire but also my spiritual horizons.

I did not realize then the therapeutic connection between the breathing and the singing. Singing was a powerful distraction from the pain and misery. I would be exhausted after rehearsals and Sunday services and sometimes more painful. Yet, I felt better! How could that be? What was really going on?

Some of my soul astrologers contend that my voice is my connection to Source. In recent years, I have learned that my voice takes many forms—thanks to *justPaula,* the storyteller who inspired me to become a poetess in 2005 and to complete this book in 2014.

I kept on singing throughout the therapies and setbacks, even a few at church. But I never stopped. It has been more than 20 years. Singing is the one thing I have done for the longest time in my life! Energy medicine will probably turn out to be #2!

Singing with purpose and meaning helped everything. My pain was more tolerable and, over time, lessened. The dysthymia and depression could often be discharged with the vibrational medicine of my voice. Mostly, I sang sad songs. Most people think this makes you sadder. It helped me to release sadness. I could sing "motherless chile'" until I was no longer feeling motherless. Then I could sing songs of joy to announce my return to gladness.

Singing was often a breakthrough mechanism. I would sing through a difficult panic episode and release the distress I was holding. The words and melodies would soothe the savage beast. The breathing would medicate my spirit and oxygenate my body. Healing was almost always going on. I left church on Sundays with a sense of joy, peace and hope regardless of how hard I struggled to be there. Singing was my salvation.

Singing is one of the primary therapies over which I have control most of the time. My favorite pastime is still to sit at my piano and play and sing hymns and songs of faith. I am a cantor in the church, and I love to sing psalms. They are often my warm-ups and the focus of my Lenten discipline. Lent and Easter and, of course, Christmas, are precious seasons for me musically. Palm Sunday is my benchmark Sunday and my favorite ritual day, but that is part of another story.

Sing on! Sing on! Spirits of the world! Find your voice and use it to heal your heart and soul. I did. I recommend it highly. There are many forms of accepted music therapy in this new age. Find the one that best suits you if singing is not your thing. Try chanting, for example.

I also use the piano as an instrument of healing for my hands and arms and physical self. I play even when it is painful so that I can play through the pain and find a place of freedom from pain. I know this sounds contradictory. The human spirit and even the human body are full of mysterious ways to rebuild and repair.

Einstein said, "The most beautiful thing we can experience is the mysterious. It is at the source of all true art and science."

I couldn't agree more!

It would be 2013 before I would understand the impact and import of the many betrayals that sabotaged my soul's joy at every juncture—my beloved voice among the losses I would have to regain to be whole once more. I would be called to heal my anger or relinquish this most precious gift of singing. Or thank God, this is what I believed at the height of my madness and pain and disability. I sang healing melodies and lyrics with all my heart and soul and might to ameliorate the challenges of my long recovery and rehabilitation. I lived qualitatively and responsibly to tell stories of forgiveness and love. Thanks, Mommy, for playing so I could sing!

So just when I think this section about singing for the Lord is concluded, I have another revelation. This is a true case of saving the best for last!

My greatest gift of all time, also my greatest responsibility as a singer, was giving birth to another great singer, a rock star, no less! What a wonderful life it has been watching my beloved daughter, Sylver, sing her way to fame and fabulosity and even a little fortune on occasion!

For two decades, Sylver traveled around the world singing about love and stirring audiences to dance to *Freak Out* as lead singer of the legendary band, CHIC. She performed on stage at Montreux Jazz Festival and the esteemed concert series, *Night of the Proms,* in Belgium—to cite just two.

As a solo artist, Sylver has appeared on radio and TV shows and wowed fans with a #1 *Billboard* dance hit, *All This Time* in 2005. Her debut solo CD, *Place to Begin,* is a masterpiece of melodies and messages that say: *Don't Give Up (on You)* and *I Love You.* Her new CD, *The Groovement,* recorded in Stockholm, Sweden, in 2013, is scheduled for release this summer. I can't wait! Can you tell I'm a really proud mother? So log on to: www.sylverlogansharp.com. Enjoy Sylver's timeless, inspirational vocal artistry. Then tell a few friends!

It is no coincidence that Sylver's first solo in a Little Miss pageant at age four was a self-fulfilling prophecy. For sure, she would spend many days and years *Leaving on a Jet Plane* with her bags packed and ready to go. I've been with Sylver's prolific singing career from the start. It's still an "Adventure in Paradise," to quote a song by Minnie Riperton.

Singing rocks not only my world but also my dreams! Sylver's anointed voice is a gift only God could have created and entrusted to my care. This is one responsibility I welcome with open arms and heartstrings that zing with joy.

Here ends my saga about singing. Hope you enjoyed it!

Religion and ritual

Say what you want about religion, it affords a ritual experience that has proven merit. In an age where spirituality is less and less linked with religion, let me offer that we not throw out the baby with the bathwater. Religion and ritual can both be healing gifts if used responsibly.

The act of going to a sacred quiet place to worship and praise God or Allah or observe the stillness is an act of self-love. The community of saints is all of us, sinners and enlightened ones alike, as far as I am concerned. Sometimes we need the potency of a community to deepen our relationship to Source. Sometimes we need the camaraderie of like-minded others to remind us that there is a Divinity connecting all mankind and all creation.

The self-healing love embodied in religious or spiritual practices can be felt in a temple or mosque or sweat lodge or by a lake, even in a backyard or in a sun porch garden. Location, denomination or creed is not so important. Intention is paramount. I, of course, am discussing a loving intention.

For the record, I consider myself both religious and spiritual. I consider myself a spiritual being (most of the time, that is) having a human experience. I take full responsibility for my religious and spiritual beliefs and rituals that I consider healing gifts. I neither create nor find any conflict between these two types of mystical experiences.

The Dali Lama, in his writings, suggests that we literally "create" our own enemies by the thoughts we become attached to. The Buddha is quoted as saying, "All things are mind made." Food for thought!

Going to a Christian church, more specifically the Episcopal Church, has been just as tonic to my healing process as meditation and energy medicine. That is a mouthful in my complex world and a powerful truth. My ministry in the Voices of Praise choir taught me to embrace the Baptists, Catholics and all denominations in the name of Jesus. I appreciate the expanded consciousness. I actually learned to stand up and "witness" my healing miracles at evangelical choir concerts, which deepened my relationship to the Light that was growing within me.

The ritual of the 40 days of Lent and Easter Week kept me faithful to the promises of God, year in and year out. Palm Sunday became my annual evaluation day.

At St. George's, it is a long-standing tradition to walk around the church or block (weather permitting) on Palm Sunday. As a part of this ritual, the choir and congregation sing hymns and a cantor sings the liturgy. Every year, I sang the Psalm #118, heralding the call of the crowds to Christ, *Hosanna in the Highest! Blessed is He who comes in the name of the Lord!* The first few years that I was gifted with this responsibility, I sang outside with the crowd of worshippers in attendance that Sunday as we walked the walk that Jesus walked to Calvary. It was very befitting my persecution complex in the earliest years.

How I survived that walk around the church on Palm Sunday

was my baseline for the next year and my result for the present year's Lenten discipline. Sometimes I was crushed by the weather no matter how many layers I wore. Then there were later years when I incurred almost no harm at all! I was exuberant when I finally walked without injury at all! Amazing grace!

No matter the outcome, the fact that I was able to go to church and sing on Palm Sunday was a gift from God that made all the difference in my recovery and rehabilitation. It was the least I could do for a loving God who was so faithful to me.

I was healed, redeemed and resurrected in my home church where I received an abundance of love and holy prayers. I have served as Palm Sunday cantor for 18 years now! Thanks be to God!

I got stronger and stronger as the years of committing my voice to the Lord went by. My mental conditioning to alleviate careless thinking and change old habits that no longer served me was a ranking success story. I took Bible study every Wednesday, gave up unhealthy foods, revived my workout regimen and tuned my voice, all with fervor and passion.

The Lenten season was one of the few times of year I could convince myself to draw near and do it right (my healing regimen, that is) or at least close to right. The opportunity to "read, learn and inwardly digest," as my minister, Father Harris, reminded me, was integral to my spiritual growth. He also reminded me that if I made it through Holy Week to Easter, I would be changed. An insightful spiritual leader, he was always right about that.

I kept journals of my daily regimen thanks to the urgings of Dr. Adams. I added affirmations and gratitude journaling to my repertoire over time. These are good things. They all worked!

There are many kinds of rituals that support our innate need for the familiar. Our workdays and meals and Sunday church attendance are some of the best known.

I also acquired the habit of lighting candles to symbolize the white light of the Holy Spirit when I am praying. This ritual invites peace and calm—and I do remember to blow them out!

In many ways, my success with self-healing all returns to the idea of repetition. Repetition works! *Do it till you're satisfied,* a song once said. I hope that whatever religion, ritual or spiritual practice you choose serves your highest potential and the cause of lovingness for all mankind.

Pray! Believe! Trust!

I think I will open this segment with my favorite one-verse poetic ditty, a crisp and powerful play on words entitled, *You Never Was . . .*

If you don't believe in yourself
Then it doesn't matter
If nobody else does;
Cause the me
You're gonna be
Is the someone
You never was . . .

Don't let this happen to you! Pray, believe and trust without ceasing! Pray, believe and trust until something changes! Pray, believe and trust because it works!

I know what you are saying. Just when you thought I had let go of the religious talk, I start backpeddling again. Not so! These three words define the essence of *The Secret* we are learning more and more about from acclaimed author, Rhonda Byrnes. This secret is also a spiritual gift.

What I have learned is that I manifest what I pray about, believe in my heart and trust with all my might. These three dimensions of my presence to myself are integral to my ongoing healing process.

I was quite surprised to find out what some of the self-sabotaging beliefs were that held me in bondage to my careless thoughts. I was also intrigued by what I believed that was just a lie I was telling myself. My shadow side was full of negative self-fulfilling prophecies held in my wounds.

There were ideas about myself—like the "black sheep" curse—that I did not want to accept as nonproductive if viewed in the negative. There were struggles with my dis-eases for which I did not want to take responsibility—like the venomous effects of anger. There were aspects of my dis-eases I preferred to ignore or to deny that I could do anything significant to heal or relieve. For a while, I did not pray without ceasing or trust and believe that I could be panic free. As a result, I did not allow my spirit to dream the impossible dream dwelling within my soul.

Fortunately, I was inspired by books that I read and practitioners that I counseled with to reevaluate my belief systems and associated behaviors. It was very useful to reconsider my acquired values, cultural perspectives, community conditionings and institutionalized trainings. Some inconsistencies I could grasp right away. Some embedded ideas I just never thought about as causing collateral damage—like self-hatred.

So, yes, I am suggesting that it may be time for you to review your beliefs, who and what you trust and how your prayers (thoughts) manifest who you are and where you are going. There may be precious healing gems nesting inside your views and philosophies about life and living and even Health.

Do you pray for others as well as yourself? Do you pray for your enemies? Do you believe in God, the teachings of Jesus, Buddha, Native wisdom or Divine Intervention? Do you believe in your ability to heal yourself and access your inner physician? Do you believe in serendipities or the power of love? Who are you and who or what do you trust? Sorry for all the questions. Right now, I am going for the gusto in my quest to reach you somewhere deep within.

These words of encouragement about the gifts of prayer, belief and trust are offered to highlight our responsibility to make a difference in our own sacred contracts. We can each make unlimited healing choices. The resources to help us discover what works are available more than ever before in our history. In 2014, we have the Internet, smart TVs and smart phones! Technology gives us greater access to what works.

"Ask and ye shall receive" is a powerful part of the secret to claiming our fortunes and realizing our dreams. Sometimes asking is all about trusting and believing and praying out loud. Other times, asking is chanting a mantra, holding a healing intention or pleading with all our heart and soul. Sometimes asking is loving and caring for someone else in need of healing.

St. Francis of Assisi reminds us, "It is in giving that we receive, in pardoning that we are pardoned . . . let us seek not to be consoled as to console."

Sometimes our hearts' desire for asking to receive a blessing or an answer to a prayer is achieved just by being still and knowing that God is bigger.

A bit of poetry here might expound upon some of my feelings about beliefs. My treatise on this subject is called *A Matter of Belief.* This poem was inspired by the aftermath of Hurricane Irene in 2011, which not only severely damaged the roof of my house and decimated my treatment room but also put me in a very stressful posture with my bank and household insurance company. Renovations and recovery were slow and uncertain for months before peace was restored to our home. Verse one sets the tone:

A matter of belief
No ordinary thief.
Brings overwhelming grief
For which there is no relief.
A statutory beef
With that which my soul keeps.
So I gnash my teeth,
Moan and groan in my sleep
And look for answers deep
That belie the evil that seeps
Into my heart and bleeps
All the joy and dignity beneath.
So now my spirit weeps,
While overseers reap
In quantums and heaps.
I, in panic, seek
To not become weak.
Because I trusted the thief . . .
Who had a different belief.

So that I do not end this discussion on a discouraging note, let me report here that I ultimately gained a lot of spiritual strength from the destructive storm that frustrated my beliefs. When my sacred healing space—where I sit and write today—was raised and refreshed to a loftier status, I understood fully as reflected in the same *justPaula* poems that:

Only ONE holds the peace . . .
That knows no grief.
It truly is . . .
A matter of belief.

Spiritual Muscle Testing (SMT)

Finally, I get a chance to share a special gift that I have been waiting to proclaim as Gospel since I started writing this book. I have mentioned spiritual muscle testing in several chapters. I have waited until now to shed some light on what some might call a New Age subject. It is a true testament to my spiritual empowerment.

My most important lesson from the synchronicity of events that led me to energy medicine is best captured in the concept I named spiritual muscle testing (SMT). The idea is based on my experiences with a form of kinesiology known in modern psychology as neuro-muscular feedback. This measurement technique, commonly called muscle testing, suggests that while the conscious mind can play tricks on us, the body always tells the truth.

Several methods of performing the test are employed by trained professionals to access information to be used for healing purposes, e.g., trauma resolution. Many alternative medicine practitioners use muscle testing to determine brands and dosages of supplements and even food choices. I use it daily.

According to Pratt and Lambrou in *Code to Joy,* "Neuromuscular feedback directly reveals our most deeply held subconscious beliefs as conveyed through our peripheral nerves and muscles."

I am compelled to offer a little science here to illustrate the significance of this window to the Soul. I have learned a lot about the grand design of humankind. I was not surprised to discover that our bodies have unerringly accurate and complete self-knowledge.

What I uncovered from my ongoing experiments with physical muscle testing is that we also embody an innate spiritual wisdom or Intelligence with a capital "I." Moreover, this inner Intelligence is our connection to Source energy or what Chinese medicine calls, chi or jing, and what energy medicine calls the Breath of Life.

Some of us know this feeling of resonance with the Divine as the

196

Holy Spirit. Many believers in the existence of the invisible world know the felt sense of the presence of a holy and primary energy vibration as an indicator that we have help. Angels, spirit guides and all sorts of others entities tell us so.

The idea that "Spirit knows all" is not new but perhaps is not recognized as a tangible aid to our daily lives and our decision-making process. In my experience, our inherent wisdom is our greatest endowment as humans. I am grateful that energy medicine allowed me to take physical kinesiology a step further. Our physical muscles and our spirituals muscles work together, naturally and effortlessly.

SMT is mostly a catch phrase for our knowing, right-brained self. On a grander scale, SMT is the guidance system that informs our soul's desires. Tapping into this path of knowing can yield amazing results that make life more efficient, productive, satisfying and self-healing.

So when I am asked why I chose energy medicine, I can say with confidence and courage that my spiritual muscles led me to it. Somehow I knew it was the right thing! Or, I prefer to say, *God knew.* Even when I was sitting on the floor in my first polarity therapy class propped up on pillows and in severe pain, I knew I belonged there. The confusion still lingering in my brain from my most recent panic attack and the drugs permeating my blood stream did not cloud my knowing. The journey would be long but clear.

Upon reflection, finding that place on the classroom floor was my first miracle. Divinity smiled on destiny. The dancer in my soul led me to the healer within.

I have my own special method of accessing SMT that is rather unique to my bodily injury history. The left side of my body sustained the most severe injuries, especially my shoulder. So when I started to practice physical muscle testing, my left arm taught me a thing or two about how to interpret the "yes" or "no" questions with directional or vibrational movements or both.

An affirmative response brings my arm close to my heart and sometimes causes my hand to shake vigorously. A negative response moves my arm away from my body—sometimes gently and sometimes strongly. There are occasions when my right arm gets in on the action. The emotion in the testing response is often quite amusing. Initially, I observed my Intelligence at work as I practiced. Finally, I accepted the system my inherent wisdom gave me.

My daughter has branded my method of muscle testing the "Ask your arm! Or ask one of your body parts, Momma! Or ask something!"

While that last variation may be a little suspect, I appreciate her confidence in my ability to use this gift of discernment responsibly.

There are some instances when my feedback mechanism gives me the answer to a question I did not even ask but had the potential to ask, before I asked it. The familiar bodily responses stay ahead of me a bit and shake mightily until I bypass that unhealthy purchase in the grocery store. Some of my soul inquiries are answered in my core. My midline arises for no apparent reason. Or I get a knot in my stomach. Sound familiar?

So every time I was presented with a new supplement, fragrance, potion or powder to consider as a part of my healing regimen, I used muscle testing to make my choices. Sometimes, my Intelligence said "yes" or "no" before I could finish the test. My knowing self hit the jackpot most of the time.

In 2014, I use physical and spiritual muscle testing for everything, all the time, ad nauseum. Testing every little thing is how I practice. I believe it sharpens this intrinsic skill. Some days I refrain from any conscious use of this amazing gift, creating space for Spirit to speak without any prompting from me. This is when I feel my High Priestess and Goddess energy blossom, inform my Soul and direct my bliss.

Pratt and Lambrou give an excellent description of how to

perform muscle testing in their book, *Code to Joy,* and in videos on the Internet.

Read! Read! Read!

This example of gifts with responsibilities is dedicated to Oprah Winfrey. It is probably the shortest section I will write. In some ways, it is the most important.

I could have accomplished very little had I not been willing to read, read, read. So many foreign and confusing concepts taxed my mind and my understanding of most of the ideas that I hold to be sacred and inviolate. Yet, somehow, I am better for it.

My journey with books has also been an intriguing spiritual unfolding. I seldom chose book titles; I let them choose me. Many books came into my awareness that made no sense at all in the moment they appeared. I read them anyway. I believe I was guided to do so. Some books came to me so that I would give them to someone else to fulfill their sacred healing contract.

I am indebted to the many healers and authors who took the time to tell their most intimate stories and share their discoveries. I remember when I first read about the relaxation response in one of Dr. Andrew Weil's most famous works, *Spontaneous Healing.* I recall the light-bulb moment when I read Caroline Myss's explanation of grace and sacred contracts. I often meditate on Deepak Chopra's reverence for beauty as a healing principle. I reread Iyanla Vanzant's stages *In the Meantime* and take counsel from the writings of the Buddha and the Dali Lama. I am a student of the Bible and continually marvel at the usefulness of scripture and its appropriateness in spite of dogma.

I cannot say enough abut reading. It is fundamental to everything. It is a free gift. There are libraries in most cities and towns—even in the digital age. Now there are books on tape and even people who will read to you if you need assistance. There are Kindles and e-books!

Do not be afraid to read what you do not already understand. Learn something new, embrace unfamiliar ideas and preserve old, timeless traditions. Citizens of the world have an enduring responsibility to stay informed and regularly engaged in the learning process as a matter of Health Building. Reading also enhances our sense of connection to others and our understanding of their woes and joys. Whatever the driving force, read for the good of your mind and the good of mankind.

CHAPTER 11

What Do I Know for Sure?

THE LITERARY WORLD HAS BEEN OPRAH-IZED like many things. As far as I am concerned, that is okay. What she has shared with us is worthwhile; certainly, her heart is in the right place. My healing process was greatly expanded and enhanced by the information that was disseminated during Oprah's Change Your Life series in the '90s. It did change my life!

Oprah always asks of those she most reveres: "What do you know for sure?"

So I think an answer to this question is a good follow-up to the chapters on what worked for me.

It might be that green applesauce or Km or any kind of supplement would never work for you. It could be that the scent of lavender offends you (maybe your least favorite aunt wore it). It could be that you don't even believe in God or a supreme being.

I doubt, however, that you would argue too much with the following viewpoints:

1. Careless thinking kills/costs.

2. Forgiveness is a gift you give yourself.

3. Love is the answer.

What I know for sure is that there is a 99 percent chance that these things are 99 percent true! So here goes. Here are my stories about these ideas.

1. Careless thinking costs/kills.

It is hard to imagine a life with positive thoughts all of the time. This is why the "committee" or the "internal judges" in the subconscious mind get away with so much. It is considered okay in our culture to think negative thoughts about most anybody and anything as long as you do not act upon them. Until very recently, thinking was not understood to be action. Then quantum physics came into the picture and changed that aphorism.

"Talk is cheap," most folks say, and most think thoughts are cheaper still because no one hears them. It is all in our minds. In reality, more time is spent wasting than developing our minds. Whether valid, useful or sinful, random ideas and information are permitted to run rampant in our minds, in all our conversations and even our professional deliberations. Careless thinking is perhaps our greatest travesty as a people.

As I think, so I believe. As I believe (sow), so I reap, the Bible tells us.

To recover my wholeness, I had to retrain my thoughts almost as much as I had to retrain my muscles. It took a lot of concerted effort and self-trickery to get through all the layers of beliefs about my being that were contributing to the stubbornness of my dis-eases.

My first stabs at mind reorientation, I'll call it, involved the simple act of *noticing* the quality of all my daily thoughts. Quality had to do with whether or not my thoughts were suggesting anger, fear or hatred of myself or someone else. Rage was a separate category all by itself.

During one of my Lenten disciplines, I decided to count the cost of my careless thinking. I came up with the brilliant scheme to collect a fine from myself for every anxious, angry or rage-filled thought. Angry words cost more, especially cussing out loud.

Every angry thought cost me a dime, every rage-filled outburst cost a quarter and simple negativity cost a nickel. I was having a really hard time with angry thoughts and rage leading to panic attacks in those days.

Needless to say, it was totally bothersome to actually pay attention with due diligence to every thought throughout the day. It was truly surprising to realize how costly my faulty brain waves had become. Way, way too much of my time, effort and energy had succumbed to the rantings of a crazy person. I would sometimes try to remember to go stand in the mirror and watch the rage on my face. It was horrifying to witness. It was useful to observe it.

Brain baggage has a way of hanging on long after an event creates it. It is the computer inside the brain! So there I am six months later still ranting about the way I was treated by this one or that one. A mind possessed is a terrible thing!

The worst part of this exercise of disciplined thinking was not my rather generous Lenten offerings but the counterproductivity of my mental rantings that was revealed. No wonder I was tired all the time. I was always feeding my addiction to negativity.

The nickels, quarters and dimes did make a difference though. By Easter week, I noticed a change in my thought offerings and my presence in the world. The constant attention to and casting out of unhealthy thoughts had an overall impact of disabling the constant committee chatter. Negative self-talk had been confronted head on and caught in the act, bought and paid for. And thus it became a part of my past.

With the decided decrease in negative thinking after the Lenten exercise, I found peace. Imagine that? I recognized a power I was giving away that was diminishing my capacity to express Health.

I also noticed how I felt about the people in my life. I observed my thoughts about them as a portal to learning more about my view of myself. As I explored the complexities of my mind, I realized that I needed support systems to maintain a positive result. So I developed another strategy that proved to be enlightening and effective in resolving the struggles with negativity and old habits.

Around the same time that I was in the throes of the Lenten lessons and counting costs, I had a reading by an astrologer friend of mine on the deck of my house at Flagler Place. Among other intriguing aspects of my personality that he exposed through my birth date and the alignment of the stars, was the idea that I was inflexible. Me? Never! But my stargazing friend was someone that I trusted. So I choose rather to embrace his oracling instincts and see how I could reconcile the need to be more flexible. It was a thought worthy of further investigation.

Of course, the first thing I had to do was to figure out what this meant in terms of my behavior. How and when was I not flexible? I'm ashamed to say it did not take long to find a good example.

I was just beginning to schedule sessions with clients to hone my craft as a student practitioner of polarity therapy. Well, I am a person who is always on time. While that may be an annoyance to some people, it is usually a feather in my cap. I am very happy about this trait.

However, seeing clients changed everything. They almost never kept their appointment times and often cancelled at the last minute or wanted to reschedule for reasons that were not paramount to me. This was a disaster waiting to happen if I was not flexible enough to roll with the punches. No matter the cause, it was never going to benefit me to get upset every time a client was late or called to reschedule. It was just not a worthwhile investment of energy. So every time I had the occasion to respond to a change in the plans of my clients, I reminded myself consciously to be flexible, as a mental suggestion. The simple act of repeating an idea again and again in my mind made it real, along with providing me with the experience to support it.

I stopped taking offense to disturbances of my comfort level that did not need to be so. I made a choice not to be offended. I behaved my way into it, as Dr. Phil likes to say. If I was going to have any peace as a practitioner of the healing arts, I needed to make this choice, successfully.

I now take pride in the fact that I am empowered to go with the flow as they call it in 2014. Flexibility was a personal attribute that someone like me needed to acquire considering my tendency to be rigid in my striving for perfection. It was not my way of being in the world. The A student was always well prepared and easily frustrated by others who lagged behind.

I took this idea of a new flexible me a bit further and applied it to other concrete activities in my life. My favorite example is the way I reconciled my distress over always being early or on time for choir rehearsal. I often found myself on time and by myself.

After years of waiting alone, I began to feel a little crazy. Surely I did not need to sit and wait on others to show up at the same place week in, week out and not do something about it—especially since it had become a real sore spot for me. So I did something about it. I decided to be late.

This radical decision required a new thought process. The idea was actually fun after a bit of practice. I just decided to reduce the length of my wait by coming a little bit later than I normally did. To wit, I made an adjustment. If rehearsal was at 7:30, I usually arrived around 7:15. On my new regimen, I arrived at 7:45, when everybody else was arriving. I was only 15 minutes late and saved myself 30 minutes of waiting and annoyance. I couldn't do anything about my fellow members so I did something with myself to ameliorate the angst.

However hard it was to learn how to be late and to alter my

thoughts on the subject, I came to realize that flexibility was becoming my new way of being in the world. I already knew how to be on time.

I realize that I could have just accepted the 30-minute lead time with a peaceful spirit or used it for a brief mediation. I chose something else that was a little more intriguing to me. Any one of these choices would have required a change in my thought pattern to effect a change in my behavior.

Like everything else, following my new pattern was just good ol' repetition. Barely a day went by that I did not repeat the words, "I am flexible," over and over. Affirming my commitment on a daily basis and looking for situations to discover more opportunities for growth was my daily bread. The choir rehearsal routine was just one application of the newfound discipline of reciting mantras and affirmations.

Inventing my flexible self was an exercise in cleansing that grew into something very empowering as the years passed. I developed the ritual experience of selecting two or more buzzwords or life themes or affirmations each year at Lent from then until today.

As I complete the final draft of this book, my 2014 Lenten precepts and prayers: "Trust, Obey (quickly) and Surrender," are essential to my forward progress. It will take all three of these powerful intentions to fulfill this sacred contract.

After Katrina, my foci were compassion and harmony. I questioned my own compassion when I felt powerless in the face of all the pain and panic that was ricocheting throughout the world. I was mesmerized by the potential for a critical mass of post traumatic stress disorder sufferers and displaced souls longing for a place to rest and recover. I felt their pain and wailed inside to even think for a moment about their losses on all levels of being-ness.

I thought, as an African-American as I watched New Orleans (where my brother and his family live), "Those are my people. Why do they suffer so? Why am I so paralyzed?"

It was hard to consider the dark night of the soul that would follow this experience for many. Yesterdays came to stay!

Then *It* happened! Even as I write these stories almost nine years later, I am not certain about what *It* is that orders my steps. Yet, all of a sudden, one morning in late August 2005, I felt energy swirling around in my head calling me to get a pen and paper and write. Words came forth like a shower of healing love. Poetic stylings that told all of my life stories and earth school dramas spilled out with clarity and truth and surprise endings of which O. Henry himself would be proud. As of 2014, I have written over a hundred poems.

I still remind myself constantly to hold in my heart of hearts those who suffered from the devastation of Katrina. In many ways, they not only defined my journey but also opened the floodgates (no pun intended) of my new beginning as a writer. I am forever indebted to their pain.

The strategies of affirming higher thoughts and assessing a fine for acts of negativity were ideas for managing my tendency for unhealthy activity in my conscious or subconscious life. They are only tools. Strategies must be supported by a sincere desire, I believe, for self-improvement. These methods are not entertainment no matter how creative the process. The heart center must be involved. The conscious will must be engaged. The courage to change must prevail with no doubt. Otherwise, the change may never be integrated into our being. Practice without the potency of desire is for naught. I believe this to be gospel.

So what do I give up with all this positive thinking? This is the usual default thinking, is it not? I have to respond, "I gave up nothing of value, really."

Perhaps I miss the hours spent degrading my enemies and gossiping with friends and plotting revenge. Or not. After all, old habits die hard.

Thinking and talking about people and things is, after all, a large part of life itself. Freedom of speech is the American Way.

And, of course, talk is necessary to negotiation in the 21st century. Criticism is an essential component of growth. This is true of constructive criticism. However, most thinking that relates to formal critique is anything but constructive. Very often, what comes out is vain, argumentative and ego-driven.

When positive thinking becomes a way of life, we give up the opportunity to be unkind. Who could be that nice all the time? It is not about being nice. It is about living in Spirit from a place of love. Think about it! Oh no! I said the word, "Think!" But don't think carelessly. Think responsibly whenever you can. It could save your life or the life of a friend. It could change the world. It could bring peace.

I found the most profound reason for healthy thinking in the writings of Deepak Chopra. One of the primary principles of his book, *The Seven Laws of Spiritual Success,* is to live without judgment. There are many ways to interpret this advice. For me, it became a way to release my mind and to have more physical and spiritual energy. When I began to notice the amount of time, effort and energy I was expending every time I made a mental judgment, I was astonished. What a waste!

I could spend 20 minutes pondering an unimportant situation or even an important one, starting with, "Well I don't think . . ."

I'll add a few examples:

- "I don't know why she is wearing red hair! It really does not look good on her. What was she thinking?"

or

- "Now you know, Pastor's wife's skirt is just a little too short! She needs to let that thing down a little. Girlfriend, I think she might have a little floozy in her."

or

- "Why doesn't he get a real job? Who does he think he is? Trying to make a living playing music? He'll never make any real money! And so on, and so on . . .'"

Maybe the person in question making the judgments is upset because her "do" is fading or because she always wanted to wear red hair. Maybe the next person also wants to wear her skirts a little bit shorter but doesn't have legs as cute as pastor's wife. Maybe this same person has a little "floozy" in her as well. In example #3, maybe the observer had parents who refused to let him play music for a living or even at all!

Whatever the reason, it was all unnecessary, careless thinking that amounts to nothing but a tired brain. All the time spent dwelling on pastor's wife's legs is a reflection of the judgment-maker's own inadequacies. "Da judge" could have been working out to get some muscles in her own legs. Better yet, she could just have observed pastor's wife without judgment at all and saved some energy.

When I say, "All the time spent . . .," I mean it literally. Like everything else, unhealthy habits cost valuable time and resources. In a world of constant overload, there is no space for this misuse of human potential.

Careless thinking is the true meaning of the UNCF (United Negro College Fund) slogan, which I quote often, "A mind is a terrible thing to waste."

This motto also reminds me to quote one of my own poems with a Rudyard Kipling title, "If." Consider, for a moment, the opening lines:

If you are dwelling on falling
Then you can't be rising.
And all your results
Must be most surprising!

As I mentioned earlier, Iyanla Vanzant, in her writings, offers the concept of re-languaging. When I first heard it I thought, "Now that is a clever idea!" If you can apply "re" to most anything, meaning "do again" or "do over," why not language?

How we speak about our life experience is often screaming out our issues. My favorite example of "re-languaging" that Iyanla suggests is saying, "temporarily out of cash," to replace the concept of "broke." The thought that being out of cash is "temporary" worked well for me. It always meant help was on the way. What an easy conversion from the worst—"I don't have nothing and nothing is coming!" The words, "temporarily out of cash" softened the associated anxiety, just like magic. Suggestion works. And, indeed, Iyanla, had a magical idea about how we express our presence in the world.

From this awakening about careless thinking, problems became challenges and overcoming them became spiritual growth. I went on to appreciate other ideas about careful word selection and re-languaging my experiences from Gary Zukav, Caroline Myss and, of course, good ol' energy medicine.

I liked thinking about my struggles as lessons in earth school and my worst experiences as holy moments. I liked the idea of a sacred contract as the focus of my life. It was another way of being gentle with myself and softening my anxious responses to so-called negative events and thoughts. Re-languaging was a lifesaving change in perception, the champion of mental stumbling blocks.

"The way I see things is the way I see things," most people say. "It is impossible for me to change my perception."

The idea that something is impossible is the most profound insult to the human spirit that I know about.

I think the Buddhists are recognized as the vanguards of holding perception without detriment. Their corollary between struggle and enlightenment leads the way for someone like me to see dis-ease and healing as a pathway to empowerment. The ability to alter my perception of a so-called "negative" event lifts the responsibility to elicit a negative response. Rather, this humbling way of seeing and thinking about life resonates like a deep cleansing when I embrace it with honesty and trust.

When I am asked about my pain in 2014, I respond, "I have pain, but my pain perception is almost nil."

With all the things that worked and alleviated my pain, I learned that my ideas about it were as important as my experience of it. The pain was worse when I was "mad" at it. This idea about pain was especially true and effective during my therapy sessions. Once I learned to love my painful muscles and to not curse them, they began to heal!

So I learned to understand pain as the armor of anger that I no longer needed. The angst in my heart held the pain in my body. I had to let anger go to access freedom from pain. Anger was, of course, not the only perpetuating factor even though it was a constant aggravating factor.

I changed my perception of the relationship between my experience of anger and my dis-eases, especially the experience of pain and panic. The result was a change in my response to crises and a change in the level of the pain I felt. Amazing grace yet again!

Much like I changed my careless thinking habits, I changed my way of handling conflict, which had been a lifelong weakness. I acquired the mind-set that to the extent my anger was under control, my potential for my dis-eases to become worse was curbed. It was under control.

Don't think it was easy or even as simple as I make it sound in the moment. Repetition and practice, behaving my way, successes and failures were all part of the gradual retooling process that took months, years and concerted effort. My experience of transformational ideas is still a work in progress in 2014.

The benefits of what I learned are immeasurable primarily

because of what I discovered along the way. The act of engaging my own energy in a more positive manner changed my awareness of myself forever. Once awareness shifts, everything else shifts with it.

In energy medicine training, practitioners are instructed to ask clients, "What are you aware of?"

This inquiry is a way of teaching them to notice and engage their healing resources. Awareness exercising is another door to accessing the Health Within. It is useful in helping sufferers acknowledge what they do not want to confront in an environment of support. This introspective inquiry is another way of asking the higher self to identify what needs to be healed to reinforce and prepare for what comes up.

Now the greatest behavioral challenge of all: How do I learn to create zero tolerance for yelling and screaming and abusive language and flaring fights. This was the tip of the iceberg. In truth, one of my earlier triumphs, and one of the most precious, was creating a new bottom line for my emotions. I've saved it for last because it is a lifesaver.

Years of anger, frustration and panic had left me on the edge of my being most of the time. It was almost impossible to get through any disagreement without a yelling match. I just went into anger so easily. It was a knee-jerk reaction that was totally out of control. I had this tendency for much of my life, but it became worse when I was living in constant pain and struggling with authorities. Flaring-up in anger or frustration was one of my worst perpetuating factors. I knew it had to stop.

Starting with Sylver, I worked my way through this tremendously debilitating behavior. Over time, we both overcame almost all of our experiences of vociferous and volatile discussions. We agreed that such behavior was just not tolerated. Establishing a "no screaming allowed" pact made a significant difference in the harmony of our relationship and our ability to assist each other with our sacred contracts. Because we were willing to change our perception of how we could be, our relationship prospered. We are not finished, but we have accomplished a lot.

Some would ask, "What comes first, the change of thinking, the change of language or the change of perception?"

The truth about what I am saying remains: "Careless Thinking Costs and Kills. This I know for sure!"

I started this section by saying how hard it is to imagine a world without negative thoughts. It is exactly what we must do—imagine it!

2. Forgiveness—A gift I gave myself.

Ideas come and go and some just drop in your lap. This is the literal truth about how and when I got the message about forgiveness. Say what you want about TV talk shows, a lot of useful stuff gets proclaimed along with the propaganda.

I don't recall the name of the African-American female psychiatrist who said it, although I do have a notable recollection of her standing up in the studio audience on the *Rolanda Show* and offering the sage counsel, "Forgiveness is a gift you give yourself."

It was one of the holiest of my holy moments. Instantly, I *knew* the answer. I thought, "Fewer angry reactions could yield fewer pain reactions, if I would only forgive, or at least, think forgiving thoughts."

It was then and is now the hardest of the things that worked to implement. I was hardwired for anger and rage after years of panic, pain and abandonment. I was mad at just about everybody for just about everything and I felt justified in my anger. I had been abused by many and had suffered a lifetime of envy and mistreatment by many. My past was not a pretty picture.

One of my challenge warriors asked me, "Who did this to you?" in one of our most profound healing sessions. I knew that she knew that I was holding major travesties against my spirit that became internalized as physical pain and energetic distortions.

Yet, my determination to overcome my debilitating maladies won out. My inner *knowing* realized that very day that the pretty lady psychiatrist was right. I could help myself if I could manifest the Gift of Forgiveness.

Another beginning was upon me. My initial questions were, "Who do I start with? Who is first in line to help me get this magical gift?"

You know the answer to this one. My beginning place was to forgive myself. My self-directed anger was my health enemy #1!

I had no idea how immersed I was in self-loathing as a conditioned response to childhood abuses. If only I could re-language the name-calling bullies in my cellular memory so that I would not hate my light-skinned blackness or my silky hair. If only I could change the threats to steal my lunch money because I was a child of privilege. If only I had learned how to defend myself and not to run and hide. The list of "if onlys" could be my next book.

If only they had believed me when I said I was in pain, if only they had brought me a heater, if only they had not rallied against me when I fell. If only I had not had the archetype of a pioneer. If only I had not had a sacred contract with healing.

The latter two "if onlys" turned everything around for me. Once I learned that there was a purpose to everything under the sun, I was forgiven. I was no longer a hopeless mistake in my own eyes. All those people who made up the "if onlys" were not the enemy. I was not responsible for what others did to me. I was only responsible for what I did about it. So what, if I was always ahead of my time, misinterpreted, misjudged, yet leading the way for others in need of healing?

I learned to accept myself with all of my differences. After all, that is what many abuses are, differences that are misunderstood. Some of the light stuff, the minor hurts could be reconciled with the knowledge that people hate what they do not understand. Sadly, embedded ignorance is part of our cultural conditioning and our spiritual wasteland.

It was not their fault that they hated me so and felt justified mistreating me. It is probably what they were taught by significant others. Hatred is a learned behavior in most societies and in dysfunctional families as well. I think almost everyone I have asked the question of has admitted to being on the receiving end of acts of unwarranted hatred or what I call "secondhand pain" imposed by others.

I must forgive the "haters" for they know not what they do. How sad it is that so many people have learned to hate instead of to discover something new. How sad that the range of their compassion is so limited. How sad that human beings have not figured out that hate destroys. How much sadder it is that the damage caused by the slow drip of careless thinking goes unsung. I will not be guilty of the same!

The significant other abuse and on-the-job injuries were major "if onlys" that yielded powerful forgiveness opportunities for me. It took serious trauma therapy and body psychotherapy to unleash the harm to my psyche and my spirit. I came to the point in my healing where seeking the capacity to let go of past hurts from my being so that I could move on was as necessary as breathing. Forgiveness was the gift I had been waiting for.

In many ways, forgiveness for me was another change in perception. However, it happened, an act or thought of forgiveness always made a difference. This healing concept truly was a profound way to get over it or make it better inside. Forgiveness softens the heart of darkness.

There are many books on the subject of forgiveness, and anger management classes are everywhere. Consider it. This could be the gift that you have been waiting for. Maybe you will have a healing epiphany as I did.

Forgive your own trespasses and the trespasses of others as we ask of our Creator in the Lord's Prayer. Forgive yourself for being imperfect in the eyes of man; we are all works in progress. In the eyes of our faithful Source, we are perfect even with all our imperfections. Forgive your enemies if you can or just keep them close if you can't. Forgive! Forgive! Forgive! It can save your life. Forgiveness is an act of love.

3. Love is the answer

I suppose your first question might be, "Love is the answer to what?"

That would be a good question. In my world, the answer to this question is, "Everything!"

The next question is then, "How could that be?"

Let's explore and discover.

I believe an act of love is a good response to any situation I may encounter. For example, if I am loving to only myself, I am better off. If I am loving to all concerned, all are better off. Simple? Simple!

This idea does not mean that I kiss it and make it well. It means that I make a loving choice.

Perhaps my interpretation of what had happened is way off base. An act of love says, "Let me consider another alternative and see through the eyes of compassion for my brother's dilemma. Perhaps I understood wrong. Perhaps I saw wrong? Or perhaps I saw correctly."

It is still a healthier choice not to allow the injury to take me out of myself into yesterday. Love is the most worthwhile choice.

I learned the lesson about what is worthwhile from my brother, John. When we were children, he noticed that I hardly ever prevailed in arguments with our mother and I was always a mess afterward. In his opinion, my extremely emotive response pattern was a waste of time with a costly outcome. Spoken like a true prep-school pragmatist, John argued vociferously and passionately that my arguments with our mom were not worthwhile. I rejected his advice then and doubted the veracity of his claims. I have since come to appreciate the value of his assessment. I learned much later in life to listen to our mother with quiet attention.

Acts of love are all that matter in life. It would take me decades to implement this idea, but finally I got it.

What you love, you integrate. What you integrate, you perpetuate. For instance, my love for dancing was always an integral part of my whole self. When I needed to dance again, this healing place was inherently available. I was intrinsically motivated by something that I loved with my whole heart. Now I am encouraging others to dance their way back to health or perhaps to prevent dis-ease. Our passions have healing power.

I had not read O. Henry, Blake or even Shakespeare in 40 years until I started to write this book. Langston Hughes is the only real constant from my early years. Even Browning was a distant memory. However, "Love is not love that alters when it alteration finds" is my new truth.

These words I have recited with such fluidity with several clients in recent years, such that Elizabeth Barrett Browning could have been whispering in my ear. This verse from her famous sonnet came through with so much clarity that I was amazed at the conviction with which I spoke. In my opinion, we love what we hold in our heart.

Love reorganizes things. The Breath of Life is this kind of love.

The Breath of Life sends the command to restore order and to access the Health Within. The energetic midline arises. Balance and harmony are manifested.

An act of love asks, "Will it hurt" before speaking or taking action. Advice and assistance from a loving heart remembers to ask. Careless thinking allows us to say anything that comes to mind even when we know a person is feeling bad. A loving choice does not hurt in any way that is lasting.

Love is not about being right or wrong. It is about intention and circumstances. Sometimes a close hug is appropriate; sometimes it is not.

Sometimes money solves the problem. Sometimes more money just makes bad matters worse.

Sometimes we just don't know what to do.

Love is most assuredly the answer if an alternate choice is harmful to oneself or others. Harm has a way of transmuting any loving intention that is a farce into painful trigger points.

Love is not fickle, for sale, conditional or earned. It is the eternal truth about who we are and whose we are. It is the first and last commandment of a magnificent Intelligence that first loved us. Christ is a good example. Buddha is a good example. The Dali Lama is a good example. You and I are good examples. We are all examples of love in progress.

Love is the one thing that should grow the fastest and strongest as we evolve and fulfill our sacred contracts. Paradoxically, love is the ultimate challenge and the ultimate truth. "Love is the Answer," I say without equivocation.

Love is prayer warriors at your bedside, smiles that make you feel welcome and dinners you did not have to cook. Love is a hand to hold in the good times, a telephone call when you are feeling alone, and a lifeline to rescue you from the edge of night.

We have a responsibility to love and are accountable for what we call love and for what we say and do in the name of love. These sentiments about love apply to our thoughts and our behaviors. Love is our greatest gift with responsibilities.

If you are reading this book, you are loved whether you know it or not. There is a Source guiding you to stay engaged in Life. You are reaching within and without at the same time. You are loved.

Of course, there is a justPaula poem. My *Love Is the Answer* poem, written in 2012, is the final entry in my new collection of poetry soon to be released. I offer here the two closing verses:

> LOVE is the Answer.
> Go spread the Good News.
> Let bells ring and chime aloud
> To get rid of those blues.
> Find some way to share
> How consciously . . .
> We must be aware.
> Of man's inhumanity . . .
> That leads to disrepair.
> How can we sleep at night?
> And act like we don't care.
> There are too many . . .
> Whose cupboards are bare.
> Where is the Love . . .
> That is available anywhere?
> Where oh where? My beloved, My dear?
>
> LOVE is the Answer
> This you can trust.
> Even when madness . . .
> Makes things look like a bust.
> Believe in ITs power.
> IT is tried and true.
> And so, today,
> I send LOVE to YOU!
> LOVE is the Answer,
> Whatever you do.

CHAPTER 12

What About Yesterday?

FOR THE MOST PART, YESTERDAY IS THE PAST. It is what I hold most dear and what I live in fear of at the same time, kind of like a parallel universe. Yesterday reminds me from whence I came. It speaks of all the major players along the way—mom, dad, sister, brother, grandmother, pastor, best friend.

Yesterday is a necessary part of today and tomorrow. And, yet, it is a place where the past meets the Resistance of the future. It is a holding space for all my dramas and things I cannot change.

But change was a must when my mind was filled with thoughts that kill and cost my integrity. I needed a new mind. When my heart was filled with hatred and malice, I needed to create a clean heart. When my body became toxic and painful, I was determined to cleanse and heal. When my spirit was stuck in darkness, I was called to seek the Light. Thank God!

Scripture tells us, "Weeping endureth for a night, but joy comes in the morning." If our individual or collective lives are at war with the laws of nature, then we must seek harmony with all creation. All of us must manifest peace on earth.

Yesterday is also a bountiful legacy of life lessons and opportunities for spiritual growth. Nostalgia tells me to remember when and then I smile or frown; either is okay. Even the "bad stuff" is in the past, or is it? That is the million-dollar question!

Time and space sometimes get a little fuzzy, and yesterday tries to get a foot in the door again. Tomorrow seems to be forever away in a moment of transition like that. Some call it crazy. Some call it mental. Stuck in a time warp, the spirit longs for clarity of intention from the world at large. Thoughts of yesterday may seem like the safest place to the soul inside. Yesterday is sacred space to those weary for connection, separated from love.

Yesterday is the edge of the precipice. It is pain so deep that a cure does not make it right. The divorce is final, but my heart is still broken. The black eye is no more, but my soul is still fractured. The morning sun has risen, but I know that terror will come again in the midnight hour.

Yesterday is imprisoned potential, stolen innocence, ancestral woundings and the angst of lifetimes. It is the "committee" that never stops telling me that I am not good enough, the scars that did not get an opportunity to heal, the prom I missed, the parents who argued, the spouse who deceived me. Yesterday is broken promises, dreams deferred, crises, griefs and sorrows. It is the memories I long to relive and those I choose to forget.

And yet, for me, yesterday is the light in my father's eyes. There was a time that I thought my life would be over when it came time for my father to cross over. He was my friend, my mentor and my colleague for most of my early career as an education professional. He was even my boss shortly after I got out of college. Together, we established a consortium of historically black colleges from the ground up.

When my dad was in his 80s and I was studying polarity therapy, he was my ten-session client. It was a very important phase of my training. All of the dimensions of my relationship with my father were blessed.

People who knew (or thought they did) about my relationship with my father often remarked that I would not do well after he was gone. But the Creator had a better closure in mind. When my father had gone home and I was left to remember his gentleness and his unconditional love, I could see only his smile in my mind's eye whenever I thought of him. What a wonderful legacy! All I had to do was summon my memory of him and there would be a loving smile telling me that I was okay. How ironic, even in death, he loved me best.

So I was not able to be sad when I thought of him. There was nothing sad about our relationship. Outside of a few spankings as a deserving youngster, he was the best dad ever. I was the luckiest daughter ever. The yesterdays he gave me were filled with joy and smiles to remember for a lifetime.

Yesterday is graduations, summers at the beach, smooches in the drive-in, more graduations, first loves and losing my virginity. It is Grandmother's Thanksgiving turkey and the birth of my namesake.

Yesterday is a break, a siesta, if you will, from the challenges of the present. In the world of overwhelm, yesterday is peace. The lines become blurred in our linear experience.

Yesterday is things I understand now, things that make me go "hmm" and things that make little sense even when I think I understand.

Yesterday is a colored man who births a Negro then becomes a Black man and births an African-American. Yesterday is the ascension of Christ, the awakening of Buddha and the Dali Lama's exile.

Yesterday is prologue. Sometimes that means I see where I have gone and how far I have come. Sometimes it means I see nothing but destruction and devastation day in and day out with no relief in sight.

Imagine what it must have been like on rooftops in New Orleans when Katrina brought nothing but yesterday's horrors, whether you were physically present or not. Imagine the Sudanese waiting to be murdered with no hope for salvation, the warring peoples who never see tomorrow and for whom all hope is lost. Imagine those who see war as a way of achieving peace. And then as Kirk Franklin proposes in one of his insightful offerings, "Imagine it all gone."

Imagine me at peace with God and all creation.

Yesterday is faith defeated by pain and panic. There is no trust of anything, only fear of everything. The moment of truth has no truth and nothing makes any sense. Reality is distorted and disturbed by racing thoughts and flushing fluids. "Run for your life," better yet, find a new reality. You want to disappear and come again another day.

The Beatles sang it best, "Yesterday, love was such an easy game to play. Now I need a place to hide away." Yesterday is a good hiding place no doubt, yet, it is better if it is just a reference beam, a place to hold my precious times and so many "holy moments." Yesterday is a wellspring of opportunities and possibilities.

Yesterday When I Was Crazy was the epiphany that channeled this call to tell my stories. It was an idea whose time had come. It came in the middle of a storm to remind me that I was healed, redeemed and resurrected by our loving Creator. It reminded me that I am living more in the present now. It reminded me that my need to hide away was no longer prevalent or relevant to my design of myself. My self-torment was over. It reminded me that I was beginning, finally, to understand my life's experiences and my soul's journey. The title of this book reminded me that it was okay to be crazy. It was not okay to hate crazy. It was okay to embrace it and learn from it. Crazy became my friend, at last. The threat of destruction was gone.

Yesterday When I Was Crazy has become my metaphor for success and my baseline. It is more of an inside story for now. Who knows what the future holds? Or as a dear friend of mine used to say, "We'll run on and see what the end is gonna be!"

I will not say that yesterday will not come again. When it is time for the teacher to come, the student will be ready! At least, this is what I like to think.

Yesterday is my study ground. I know I can return from it better than I was. Let's call it a "field trip for the spirit." When I was growing up, a field trip was intended to aid the discovery process. Self-discovery and self-study were considered integral components of our growth and expansion as sentient beings.

Yesterday is time well spent creating history, connecting with my own personal truth and finding my way. Yesterday is victories and vicissitudes, the polarity of dark and light.

Yesterday teaches me who I am by showing me where I have been and who I have been and why. Yesterday unlocks the door to tomorrow. Yesterday enriches the present to inform the future.

"O, I believe in Yesterday," the song says with fervor and passion, "O, I believe in Yesterday."

Yesterday can be a point of no return. This reality is my greatest fear.

Yesterday says that I did nothing wrong, I was not to blame. It is not my fault! Yesterday is the dark night of the soul and the shadow of the valley of death and all that they embody. Fate or destiny, a macabre contract, a soul's choice most perplexing, whatever the cause, life is a curious mystery. And yet, Yesterday defines the magic of today and the miracles of tomorrow.

Yesterday is the perception that things past have a hold on me. It simply does not have to be so. Perception can change when experience does.

A different experience is just a faith-filled journey away. Yesterday can be told to "get a grip" and "let go" gradually with work or instantly with one of God's grace-filled miracles.

Yesterday can be reduced to just a gentle reminder of what was so that what is, can be. Gentle is the key word here. I think Shakespeare said, "Go gentle into that dark night."

Yesterday reminds me to be gentle with myself. Rather than continuously telling myself to "stop being so hard on myself," I tried a different, more positive idea.

As my years of panic, pain and suffering led to disability and discomfort in my body, I learned to use the idea of gentleness very successfully. I taught myself to live gently. That is, hug softly, clap softly, walk and talk as effortlessly as possible—gliding gently on the breath.

I applied this idea of gentleness to every aspect of my life. When I could only do three slow repetitions of a stretch or exercise, that is what I did joyfully and gratefully. At least, I could move. When I could only make it to the edge of my bed, I just did whatever I could from that vantage point. When I could sit up and make jewelry for only an hour, that is what I did—thankful for that one hour of freedom.

Over time, I became stronger and stronger, collecting one powerfully gentle healing experience after another. When it came time to write this book and the pain and disability in my hands and arms started to rage again, I pressed my pen or pencil gently against the paper. The time had come to birth the words and ideas that my spirit was unfolding. There could be no reason to fail.

There were days when yesterday tried to tell me I couldn't go on and keep writing without injury. My faith and the promise of God said, "Go gentle into that dark night; you will be safe."

Yesterday, things were different. That is all that is necessary to know. Today is full of possibilities. The things that worked told me so.

I learned to use my intention to decrease or monitor the pressure or strength potential I apply to the execution of any and all tasks. My everyday life depended on the effective distribution and management of my strength potential on a minute-by-minute basis. Perhaps, I will undertake a measurement one day. For now, my impressionistic, unobtrusively gathered data will have to suffice. It is all that I have. It is, indeed, enough. In 2014, it is my instinct to be whole and to dwell in my place of knowing the God within and knowing and finding more of *what works.*

Yesterday is the past to all that is seeking the present. Safe haven or not, *it works* in desperate times and saves souls. Yesterday is a valuable storehouse and a safe house for the spirit in times of trouble. It is a resource of mammoth proportions.

Yesterday gives hope for today and tomorrow. Ironically, when I finally understood that all the trials of yesterday held the promises of my future, I taught myself to integrate my past. I know that while I am not separate from yesterday, it is, indeed not a thorn in my side only a passageway. I can forgive myself and others and perceived transgressions. I can see God forming my missions and ministries at every turn—without justification or judgment. Yesterday becomes okay!

May all your Yesterdays lead to brighter tomorrows. May the promise of God dwell in every choice you make. May the Breath of Life support your journey.

Yesterday's choices

One of my fondest yesterdays came while I was a student at the University of South Carolina. I was given a choice between psychology and philosophy as curriculum credits for a master's degree in educational research. Even though I still did not like to read, I chose philosophy. In truth, I would like to have taken both. My psychology vocabulary is still lacking as a result.

I enjoyed the philosophy course's exercise of juxtaposing truths and pioneering ideas and defining existence. I had read most of the great thinkers from Aristotle to Thoreau in high school and college. I had a working knowledge of the scholarly wisdom of the ages. I was always intrigued by the ideas, the courage and the vision of those whose meditations shaped the world.

Much philosophical banter wafted through my consciousness as a lover of classical literature. As a high schooler, I had an affinity for the classics that drove my choices of books to read and that got me into Harvard College. (Another story.)

The catharsis I was seeking came in the form of a philosophy assignment to write a dialogue, debating two sides of a question of import. It is 40 years later, so I don't recall the title of the paper. Yet, not only did I get an "A" from my philosophy professor whom I admired a great deal, but also I was proud of the work. I learned a lot about the way I think from the exercise. The study of philosophy resonated with my being.

I did not understand it then, in 1974, but I understand today why that philosophy course was my favorite. This bit of homespun philosophy that I weave today is very telling. That I should philosophize on matters of yesterday is destiny at its best!

Perhaps, by the time that I am writing my next book, I will have found my only copy of that class paper in the recesses of my stuff. I hope the Flagler Flood did not claim this significant piece of my yesterdays.

CHAPTER 13

And So It Is!

NOW THAT MY LITANY ON THINGS THAT WORKED is somewhat concluded, I feel as though I have only scratched the surface of my bountiful experiences. There are probably many more things that worked that I have not mentioned. There are also things that did not work. Most assuredly, I learned from all my healing trials whether they worked or not.

I believe my life lessons that dwell in the realm of accepted wisdom in the 21st century rank along with the supplements, therapies and events for their healing power. I learned to monitor my thoughts and eschew pointless negativity at all costs, to think long term about my goals and dreams and to be happy in the present.

I started out with fierce resistance to this concept of positive thinking all the time. (There is now a new school of psychology called positive psychology.) Thanks to my astrologer friend, I worked tirelessly to become more flexible in body, mind and spirit. At this juncture, I know for sure that I am only as healthy as my thoughts and my daily life. A mind is a terrible thing to waste. If I had not learned this, I would have learned to regret not knowing this. I would have continued to think careless, unhealthy thoughts and perhaps missed the call to heal and fulfill my sacred contract.

Get trauma therapy if you need it! When Katrina drowned us all in anxiety and horror, our whole society and our entire beings were traumatized. There had already been trauma on a global scale triggered by 9-11 and the tsunami. It is crucial to our survival as a people to heal the imbedded trauma so that it is not internalized to our detriment for generations.

For some of the severely wounded, this kind of deep healing may appear to be nearly impossible. But I do not believe in impossible. I doubt that I would be writing any of this if it were not for trauma therapy. Thanks, Peter Levine and Roger and Tom and Charmaine and polarity and craniosacral therapy and body psychotherapy. I am deeply indebted to my trauma warriors.

There are new and exciting developments in the treatment of trauma. It is possible to resource and titrate the "re-living" process so that re-injury does not occur. A brand new world awaits those who are willing to give themselves an opportunity to feel their whole-ness again. Please consider it. It is vital to heal forward the challenges of our lifetimes so that the future can emerge without so many of the burdens of the past. Imagine your trauma gone. It *is* possible.

From my heart of hearts, I say: Treasure and respect those who represent your significant relationships and caregivers and care receivers. Live in the present moment gratefully and hold forgiveness close to your heart. Understand that the most profound wisdom you may ever know is that forgiveness is a gift you give yourself. Seek clarity and a clairvoyant sense of spiritual truth that smiles behind your eyes. Anticipate joy. Be teachable and truthful. Know when not to speak or respond. Look for the rainbow!

Another bit of advice I would like to offer is this: Look for the ones that God sends to aid you. There are angels all around!

Wherever I went on my healing journey, there was always one person waiting to come to my rescue and show me some love. Jesus, the Christ; my beloved daughter, Sylver; my Sister-in-Christ, Bernice; the therapist in the pain clinic; my sister, Camille; Charmaine; Tom—and the list goes on. Expect help to show up in your life. When you least suspect it, help is on the way.

You and I have heard all these ideas, again and again. All these principles of living well are abundantly true. True peace and healing begin in the hearts and minds of each one of us. Our willingness to do what it takes to build health and not destroy it is what matters most. All life is connected. Separation is a myth or maybe it is a lie. Be encouraged. It is an available and productive choice even when appearances belie it.

When the time comes, go back to God joyfully; it is only a crossing over at best. Think about all of us. Think of those around us and even those who came before and who will come after. Think beyond yourself. Honor the universe. All these are essential elements of a qualitative life. Live qualitatively.

When all else fails remember without equivocation that *Love Is the Answer.* Loving-kindness is. God's love is. Compassion is. Forgiveness is. Energy is. All that is, is. At all our best, we are love.

May all your life choices be acts of love for you and for all creation. Go heal and be healed.

What is the latest?

That is a good question. It depends on when this book gets published on the one hand. Just joking! "What is the latest?" will always be a valid question. Of this I am certain, even if there is little to tell.

I will be holding that thought in my mind often. I will be asking myself, "What am I doing now? What's new?"

I have not spent a lot of time lately trying to conceive my vision of my up-and-coming adventures in building health. Perhaps this writing inspires me to do so. Formulating my next power regimen is a big calling for me because I am already satisfied with my present portion of the Creator's rehabilitative genius.

I hold with gentle vigilance the idea of getting stronger and stronger no matter what! I strategically engage the limits of my physical capacity on a regular basis. I would like to try pushups again to strengthen my arms—Hmm. Thanks, Mrs. Obama for the beautifully toned arms! I am always trying to expand my breathing and to keep on dancin'. My movement exercises are designed with these major objectives in mind.

Mostly, I do maintenance. Occasionally, I get to do more. Often, I need a motivating factor, like a stimulating conversation with a colleague, friend or new client for jewelry or energy work. Ongoing conditioning crosses all parts of my life and lifestyle. Essential work therapy is continuous and essential to fulfilling my sacred contract with healing. Periods of rest, recovery and relaxation are always a priority. The stillness is my #1 guru!

Skin brushing is my latest polarity exercise. Serendipity brought this detox method to my attention while researching remedies for a cancer patient. This exercise is recommended as colon therapy in the *Energy Exercises Manual* by John Chitty and Mary Louise Muller. In energy theory, there is an interrelationship between skin, the colon and the lymphatic system. According to the instructions in the manual, the skin brushing exercise is purported to activate the colon to improve elimination, to accelerate the flow of lymphatic fluids and to impart a lustrous tone to the entire body.

For almost three years, I have practiced this exercise in the shower and tub on a daily basis. It is my new favorite detox method, and it only takes minutes, a long handled brush and a healing Intention. I have added another dimension to this exercise by circular brushing of my midline chakras as a way of tuning into my core. I found this to be a beneficial way to start my day energetically.

For the most part, right now, I am writing this book. It has become almost a full-time job. It's work therapy. Completing this sacred contract with healing holds an obsessive place in my spirit and has gained momentum and a sense of urgency. It is a very unpredictable place to live. On the days that I am not writing, I think that I should be. It is almost as if I am behind some unobtrusive deadline that knows more than I do. But this idea is not hard for me to believe at such a compelling crossroads. I am a novice on the personal storytelling forum. I am having a truly baptizing experience.

In my mind, the latest is that healing has no end of itself. It has a purpose on God's earth and in the universal macrocosm of all life, a holy calling. In my opinion, healing is our greatest teacher. The potential for regeneration is youth giving. Healing brings light in the darkness and a return to wholeness. Healing restores order and integrity. Healing ignites the Breath of Life within us. So I am dedicated to the pursuit of healing in my own little laboratory in my modest house in D.C. I am letting the writing process be my newest healing force. Only time will tell.

The Girl in the Book

And the question is, "Are you the girl in the book?" Now you may wonder why I would want you to know about this particular question at this particular time in the writing of this book. It is precisely because of the true story behind this idea—the Girl in the Book—that had a major impact on my view of completing this book several years ago when I was finishing the first draft.

Consider for a moment that this book is a living document that will change my life so significantly that I will be remarkably different from the experience of the broken woman I was when I was writing this book. Seriously consider that my healing curve could become so magnified by the successful completion of this very complex undertaking that I almost do not feel her when I read the final manuscript. In years to come, I could "forget the Girl in the Book" or reduce her to a very distant memory. *Impossible? Improbable?*

I doubt that any of these seemingly *over the top* options are plausible in my experience. It is my idea that she will always be "a trauma away" under the worst conditions and a faint recollection when all is at peace. I seriously doubt she will fade with time, healing or otherwise. But then, I try not to doubt anything that stands to help me in the final analysis. So I choose to consider that I will be so remarkably healed that "the Girl in the Book" will no longer hold my soul hostage or call my name—one fine day!

So here is the story that led to this discussion in the first place. It was not really my original idea!

I was attending a holistic healing conference, minding my own business, walking around meeting and greeting my peers. While standing in line awaiting the results of my aura imaging photography experiment, I met a woman, an exhibitor, who took an interest in my picture. She was standing right behind me in line. While we were waiting, we struck up a conversation that was centered on me. So my attention was in full focus as this stranger inquired about some important work that I was doing creatively. I immediately (uncommonly so) began to speak about the challenges of being a writer who was telling a personal story about mental illness and being crazy.

Cutting to the chase, she told me two things that stayed with me for a long time after that. One of them is the reason I am sharing this story.

First and foremost, she "saw" my books flying off shelves into the hearts of people who needed to read my story. That was all that I really needed to hear. The ego wants to win and know that it is going to win. I loved it! I needed the encouragement!

More important, she said I would not be "the Girl in the Book"—a direct quote—when I was finished writing it and putting it out. I was devastated! How could this be? What was wrong with "the Girl in the Book"? Wasn't she healed? Redeemed? Resurrected? I immediately went for the negative meaning.

The stranger, who turned out to be representing one of the local spirituality institutes, had a different idea in mind.

"You will have grown to a higher spiritual vibration when this is done," she proclaimed with total authority. "You will be different from 'the Girl in the Book'," she repeated.

When my ego recovered from the idea that I would somehow be better off when I finished and released the book, I began to question my authority to write it. Once again, I was not "good enough." It was back to the drawing board for justPaula!

Say it isn't so! It isn't so! I wrestled with this idea of "the Girl in the Book" for days after that pivotal moment in time. It was a useful metaphor for a review of my transformative healing contract. Was the sacred journey over or just beginning? Was the innocence about where I was going all these years gone forever? Did publishing my story change who I am? For months after I was told that I needed more healing—my flawed interpretation—to complete this project, I felt like I was in suspended animation.

The worst had come again! It was hard to take, but I had to realize that I would not be finished writing until I was completely healed such that I would not recognize myself anymore.

My imagination was thwarted. My ego was stunned. I did not even realize the extent to which my negative conclusion about the stranger's alarming commentary might be holding me in reserve. Rather than finding insult where there is imperfection, I should have found opportunity, potential and possibilities, enlightenment even.

There was nothing at all wrong with "the Girl in the Book" becoming a benchmark or a hallmark along the way. Who was I to say when my healing would be complete? Maybe God had bigger plans than I did. Maybe, the anointed stranger had a message that contained wisdom not easily grasped by one who had become complacent or self-satisfied. I did not want to become either.

So maybe "the Girl in the Book" was an idea whose purpose had little to do with the completion of the book and everything to do with keeping me engaged in the process of healing for the long haul. Perhaps it is yet and still implausible to think of divorcing yesterday with totality. It is necessary, however, to approach tomorrow with openness and optimism to awaken to new opportunities.

Every day is a gateway. Every day is an opportunity to find out what works and work it! Find your "Girl in the Book" who needs an ego-busting message to change her life. Or just change your life, whatever comes first!

What I have learned is that the "Girl in the Book" is constantly evolving. She continues to experiment with what works to the Glory of God and she is born anew with every dawn.

Epilogue

"ARE YOU CURED?"

I was asked this question by an old beau.

He accused me of answering a question with a question when I responded, "What do you mean by 'cured'?"

I would offer you the same inquiry.

The closest I can come to saying, "I am cured!" is to claim remission from the extreme pain that I once suffered 24/7. My wellness or health factors are probably enhanced by the fact that I do not require any medications to regulate bodily functions or to control diseases.

Just so I tell as much truth as possible, I am not ashamed to admit that I keep pain and anxiety medications in my arsenal whether I need them or not. I have not used them on a regular basis for at least eight years as of 2014. My most regular pain medications are breathwork or a session with Tom.

Sometimes my life is just about resting and enjoying nothingness. I have a tendency to over-challenge and sometimes overtax my resources. Sometimes it is just vulnerability that gets in the way. I have a lot of that. Injury is frequent for those of us with little physical strength and muscle tissues that are just happy to be in the game at all.

But life and living are worth all the trials and failures and re-trials and re-failures and successes and victories and deaths and rebirths, grieving and rejoicing. The long and extensive healing process I undertook embraced all of these components of myself. As far as I am concerned, healing was a preferred option. I guess it explains my soul's choice after all. I was really worried about that.

I am hardly ever clinically depressed or dysthymic, and I have been panic attack-free for ten years. The agoraphobia and doctor-phobia and yes, cold sensitivity, still need work, but I am making regular, measurable progress. I am rarely bedridden with intractable pain at the level of ten. I don't remember my last level ten in the past couple of years. My threshold seems to be around seven or eight and mostly five and six, even when severe aggravations occur and perpetuating factors prevail.

My recovery rate is miraculous and marvelous. It seldom takes more than three days to abate any pain cycle. Anxiety and dark days seldom take hold before I apply a remedy or treatment. Rescue Remedy, a new favorite homeopathic remedy that addresses physical and emotional trauma, does the trick really well and is seldom out of reach. I am most often in touch with what is disturbing my spirit or my body or seeking clarity and discernment for one or the other or both. If I am not in touch, I ask one of my wonderful healing warriors so I can hear myself think.

I am cured in ways that no one tradition could have manifested. My sacred contract with healing took all the muster of allopathic medicine and alternative medicine. It took all the promise of antiquity and the promise of now.

I am still seeking to understand this prodigious legacy of resources and experiences. Perhaps the real cure is somewhere therein waiting to be discovered. Perhaps the next pioneer will be you or your son or daughter and an epiphany that sets us all free. Perhaps someone you know and love will benefit from my stories in a way that profits mankind. Perhaps you will benefit mankind.

I am cured in all the ways that matter the most. I am spiritually free to think and dream as I believe with both intelligence and abandon. I am free to create my own destiny with intention and awareness. I am free to approximate normalcy so that no one has to witness my pain and suffering all the time. I am free to choose what works for me to heal my body, mind and soul.

Exceptions are okay. I also know that unanticipated events can be not so good, just okay or even great. It is also true that the Creator gives better than we can ask for. I ask only for that which supports and creates my highest good and the highest good of all creation. Affirmations also work.

I have daily challenges like the next person and life challenges as well. I work on some and pencil in others. I am peaceful and happy with my life and my lifestyle most of the time. I am grateful beyond measure and prayerful deep within my heart and soul. I am passionate and I'm still working on being unafraid to love deeply. I do still have work to do!

I love my God, myself, my family and friends and my yesterdays and tomorrows. I love my church, my religion, my spirituality and my community. I love my work therapy most of the time. I love my home, and I love my daughter and my doggies. I love life, and I want to live it!

So my elbow may hurt, and I may fall asleep after three days with this book manuscript. My spiritual partnering and my prosperity may be temporarily suspended to teach me a few things. Notwithstanding these factors, I am blessed enough for a hundred people. There are few overwhelming challenges any more. I am surrounded by an abundance of opportunities, possibilities, and love that heals.

And for polarity and balance sake, I have to say that there is trouble in the world. We are all terrorized and traumatized as peoples and cultures in America and around the globe. Too many suffering souls abuse our children and our collective resources with recklessness, greed and apathy. I wear these troubles as we all do. I pray for direction and deliverance for all peoples. I cry out for healing for all those who agonize and endure heartache and are in any way disenfranchised by man's inhumanity. I meditate on Love.

I am one little candle offering whatever Light I can in the darkness. Am I cured? I leave you to draw your own conclusions.

Yesterday When I Was CRAZY

Yesterday when I was crazy,

And my mind was full of mazes

Living in doubt about my safety;

I just danced within, without

Like a soul with no earthly clout.

Frenzied thoughts raced through each moment.

Confusion cursing every torment.

Do I live or do I die?

Dare I laugh out loud

Or do I only cry?

What took away my sacred bond

With creation's golden orb?

Why do I split from core and whole

And spin a web of fragments old?

What sight betrays my spirit's flight

Into the "dark soul of the night" . . .

And yet what wonders store
In all the places
Where the victim runs the races?
With voices yelling obscenities
At my light;
Please, yesterday, please go away,
Without a fight
And let me be
To return to me.
What does that mean?
Not exactly sure.
Perhaps, just like I was before.
"Before what?" you ask.
And so did I.
Before da' bomb inside my head
Telling me I'd soon be dead
Was taking o'er my heart's desire
For peace and love and stable fire.
Before yesterday
Became today
And tomorrow
Was just a thought away . . .

—PAULA POTTS

Acknowledgments

I T IS A HUMBLING EXPERIENCE TO FIND MYSELF in the position to write acknowledgments. It means that I have been blessed with people who care. I am honored to acknowledge all those whose guidance, love and encouragement informed my journey to the completion of this book, *Yesterday When I Was Crazy.* To all who were called to walk the walk with me, I offer my Jesus notes, my songs of thankfulness and my healing joy from the center of my heart.

The first readers of the original draft manuscript held an integral place in the manifestation of this accomplishment. Of course, Sylver led the way. She constantly reminded me that my story could help others. Sylver was in the best position of all to understand this potential. She witnessed every holy moment!

My sister, Camille, took on the preview assignment with due diligence during one of her visits to D.C. She committed several days to a careful critique of the manuscript as I quietly held her sacred space. Gleefully, she reported, "I loved your book!"

Of course, I was simply delighted to hear this.

My anointed church-Mother, Bernice Ross, gave her insightful review in stages after reading several chapters at a time. She was uniquely qualified to evaluate the details as she had lived through most of them. She prayed for me, drove me to choir rehearsals and church on Sundays, brought me dinners and Bible verses to study. Bernice and I were more than conquerors in the Christ who guided our faith-filled journey. Hallelu!

Perhaps the key motivating factor in this writing endeavor was the consistent urging of Dr. R. George Adams, my primary care physician and medical hero. He started asking me early in my recovery, "When are you going to write the book?"

Dr. Adams was relentless. Hardly a year went by that I was not asked this question with a certain sense of urgency. "When are you going to start writing?" He supported this position by prescribing journaling as a requirement of the treatment plan. Somehow he understood that the years spent recording every aspect of my healing regimens daily would be a significant part of birthing the writer-girl. What a blessing!

To Dr. Adams's faithful assistants, Eva and Angie, who held us all together throughout the years, I extend heartfelt love and thanks.

Another very special acknowledgment goes to Sylver's computer savvy life partner, Daryl Hunt, for raising the bar on my technological support system. This fact is more significant than anyone reading this who does not already know me can comprehend on the surface. His gift of a brand-spanking-new wireless MacBook (with a beautiful chartreuse cover) was an unbelievable boon to realizing a writer's dream. This gift also ignited my self-publishing capabilities. As a result, I am the proud author of my first self-published poetry book, *JustPaula—A Few Words: Inside the Mind of Panic, Pain and HEALING,* as of November 2009.

I would imagine that most 21st century writers have had the experience of losing a manuscript at some point in time—especially in this age of touchscreens and pushbutton mania. Failure to boot is indescribable!

Now that I have gotten that anguish off my chest, I can acknowledge the contributions of my very close friend, Sharon Kittrell, an expert typist. When the unimaginable horror of losing my manuscript in a devastating computer crash in January 2010 stole my joy, Sharon emerged as an angel of Light to restore my sense of direction. This experience gave new meaning to the idea of no backup! But I did have hard copy so all was not lost. It just felt like it. Retyping the manuscript was the stuff of which nightmares were made. But the Universe led me to a really special person for which I am mightily grateful.

Just a few months ago, I called on Sharon again to retype the manuscript so I could carve out each chapter rewrite individually. As a result of her skill and desire to assist—a budding writer herself—I was able to stay ahead of schedule. Thanks again, Sharon!

A consult with my wonderful friend, marketing specialist, Angela Harris, led me to enter two draft manuscripts into publishing contests, which I learned about within five days of one of the deadlines. After a few final thoughts and edits, I needed someone to convert the book files to the required submission formats post haste.

The perfect tech support was just a phone call away. Eric Williams, one of my favorite real brothers, came to my aid. The details of fonts and spacing and headers and fashion and form were reconciled brilliantly as only the Master and one of his disciples could do. A gifted "techie," Eric knew exactly what to do! His loving kindness in the hectic process was a balm to my anxious soul.

I did not win either of the contests, but my manuscripts were rendered "ready to go" to any potential publisher—soon to appear.

A major source of creative inertia throughout the past several years is the loving support and inspiration of my muse extraordinaire, Dr. Thomas P. Logan, my mother's youngest brother. Uncle Tommy and his wife, Jimi, encouraged me to keep on writing with gentle nudges just when I needed them. The constancy of their calls and letters kept me in touch with this higher calling to share my stories. I know my mom is smiling from above. I got another letter today while writing!

You will probably notice my image on the cover before you read these acknowledgements. Not bad for a camera-shy model awestruck at her first photo shoot. There are just two words for my exceptional luck with the pictures for this project—Roy Cox! Roy and his wife, Erin, are the best photography team ever!

My friend, Rhonald Angelo, set designer for the fun-filled photo shoot, brought all the right accouterments. My sister-friend, songstress, Maiesha Rashad, provided beautiful crystals from her collection to hold the space. Another special friend, Alan Kittrell, clothing designer and long-time fashion guru, gave valuable guidance on my choice of "looks" and a beautiful AK original to flaunt. It was a stellar day in the studio for all who assisted and witnessed my photographic debut.

Redhead Productions, the production company Sylver and I own, also gets kudos for styling the shoot and for arranging for hair and makeup by Ga'Mele Antoine A.

The synchronicities that landed this book in the highly skilled hands of my editor/publisher, Kathleen Barnes, CEO of Take Charge Books, is another miracle story in action. I prayed longingly for the "right" person to show up to fill this role in my journey as a writer. I knew that I would know when the perfect mentor and guide arrived—I would feel it!

Long story short, Dr. Adams referred me to his new medical associate in the alternative realm, Dr. Hyla Cass, who then referred me to Kathleen. A series of emails after these auspicious introductions, a match made in heaven was the result.

Kathleen's guidance and support through the rewrite and restructuring of the narrative were pure genius! I really did enjoy the ride! Kathleen, indeed, took charge, and I benefitted immensely as a storyteller with a sacred contract to fulfill.

Special thanks to Gary A. Rosenberg of The Book Couple, for the eye-catching, colorful and beautiful book cover and the interior design. I love it!

I am delighted to honor the sage advice of Mable Cobb, a wise woman in her 90s, who taught me to live with the courage of my convictions. As I brought closure to this project, I realized the courage it took to follow the muses and tell my stories. I also recognized the conviction it took to see it to completion. Thanks, Mable!

Mrs. Cobbs' anger management motto, though not cast in the best English, is a powerful stance on personal freedom: *I ain't mad! And ain't nobody gonna make me mad!* She lived this idea gracefully.

It is important for me to acknowledge the two organizations in which I hold membership as a polarity and craniosacral therapist, the American Polarity Therapy Association (APTA) and the Biodynamic Craniosacral Therapy Association of North America (BCTA/NA). Thanks for the standards of practice that keep us pioneering our health-building work as a community.

I humbly acknowledge all who prayed for me and cared for me when I could not get out of bed and when the look in my eyes foretold an explosion of pain and panic. Most of the time I had no idea that I would be well again. Our collective witness can perhaps save others who need understanding and compassion—and a little help to Heal.

My goddaughter, Renee; my cousins, Rose and Judy; my nieces, Dianna and Dana; my dearest friends Angel, Audrey and Bill; Pamela and Alex; my St. George's family, especially choir members past and present; my Bible Study BFF's; Lula and Margaret; my metaphysical gurus, Kathleen, Herma and Corliss—thanks for your love and support. To my attorney, Jamar Creech, Esq., thanks for your expertise, insight and oversight of this important project. To my clients, I say thanks for showing up and believing in me. To those guardians in times I may have forgotten, I plead for forgiveness.

Thanks be to God and serendipity and love ones who care, my story is told. The book is complete. *Yesterday When I Was Crazy* will have her say! Hallelu!

I acknowledge and receive this "new beginning" with an illuminated vision and an open heart. I believe in the call to fulfill my sacred contract with healing through writing. I am grateful to the "village" that carried the torch of freedom with me. I am deeply passionate about the future of *energy medicine* and my personal embodiment of the Breath of Life.

My sincerest gratitude goes out to those named in this book that were closest to the stories I tell. Your connection to my life and my healing process may appear great or small. Your contribution is significant! I have learned great lessons from the relationships, events, the good times and the bad times we shared. I sincerely hope that I have recounted with reasonable accuracy our amazing life together. Many of you were key players in my stories about *What Worked,* which is the heart of the matter and the true purpose of this book. We are soul mates, you and I.

Finally, I wish to acknowledge the God of all creation. The gift of awareness of your presence makes every breath I take precious and every step divinely ordered. Thank you for your son Jesus, in whom you gave me the message, *Love Is the Answer.* Thank you for your peace which passeth all understanding. Thank you for inspiring me to write this book and then showing me how. Thank you for all the great masters, the angels and guides who watch over me and even the perfect strangers who came along to enlighten me and inform my path. Most of all, thank you for the Oneness of all mankind. Only God could have thought of that! And so it is!

www.ingramcontent.com/pod-product-compliance
Lightning Source LLC
Chambersburg PA
CBHW052035090426
42739CB00010B/1912